GRAVEYARD
OF THE
BUDDHAS

SCOTT SHAW

BUDDHA ROSE PUBLICATIONS

Graveyard of the Buddhas
Copyright © 2025 by Scott Shaw
www.scottshaw.com
ALL RIGHTS RESERVED

Cover Photograph by Scott Shaw
Copyright © 2025—All Rights Reserved

Rear Cover Photograph of Scott Shaw
by Hae Won Shin
Copyright © 2025—All Rights Reserved

First Edition 2025

This book contains material protected under International and Federal Copyright Laws and Treaties. Any unauthorized reprint or use of this material is prohibited. No part of this book may be reproduced or transmitted in any form or by any means, electronic or mechanical, including photocopying, recording, or by any information storage and retrieval system without express written permission from the author or publisher.

ISBN 10: 1-949251-97-7
ISBN 13: 978-1-949251-97-5

Library of Congress Control Number: 2026930356

10 9 8 7 6 5 4 3 2 1
Printed in the United States of America

GRAVEYARD OF THE BUDDHAS

Introduction

Here it is, *The Scott Shaw Zen Blog 32.0,* originally presented on the *World Wide Web.* All of the writings presented in this book were written between June and November of 2025.

As was the case with the previously published volumes based upon *The Scott Shaw Zen Blog;* entitled: *Scribbles on the Restroom Wall, The Chronicles: Zen Ramblings from the Internet, Words in the Wind, Zen Mind Life Thoughts, The Zen of Life, Lies and Aberrant Reality, Apostrophe Zen, The Abstract Arsenal of Zen and the Psychology of Being, Zen and Again: The Metaphysical Philosophy of Psychology, Tempest in a Teapot and the Den of Zen, Buddha in the Looking Glass, Wo Ton' of the Blue Vision, Zen and the Psychology of the Spiritual Something, Pyrophoric Zen, Fragments of Paradox, Zen: Traversing the Entity of Non-Entity, Zen and the Ambient Echo: The Psychological Philosophy of Being, Paritical Zen and the Life Science of Becoming No Thing, Obscurist Occulto: Hiding from the Definition of Meaning, Principles of the Precepts, Left Turn at Reality Central, Zen and the Outside of the Inside, Garage Sale Zen, The Zen of Volume Destiny, Zen* and *Noted for Nothing, Zen and the Search for Suchness, Flash Point Zen, Zen and the Distinct Passageway to Nowhere, Zen and the Shadow of the Flower, Zen and the Last Call of the Illusion,* and *Blank Space Zen* this volume is presented exactly as it was viewed on *scottshaw.com* with no rewriting, punctuation, or typo corrections. From this, we hope you will receive the original reading experience.

This volume of internet ramblings is presented with the date and time listed as to when each blog was originally posted. Also, the blogs in this volume are presented from last to first. With this, we hope to present a transcendence back through time as opposed to an evolving evolution. In addition, we left out the traditional *Table of Contents* in an attempt to leave this volume with a much more free-flowing reading experience.

Okay, there's the information and the definitions. Read on… We hope you enjoy it. And, be sure to stayed tuned for the ongoing *Scott Shaw Zen Blog @ scottshaw.com.*

HE NEVER DID ANYTHING FOR ME
08/Nov/2025 07:16 AM

"He never did anything for me." And, I use the pronoun, *"He,"* as an example. You could interchange it with, *"She,"* or, *"They,"* or whatever you want.

I often hear this when people are speaking about the reason why they are not willing to do something good for someone else.

For some reason, people only seem to want to reach out their hand and do that something good or nice or helpful or whatever for someone when they feel that person deserves their help. Someone they feel has earned their help by that individual having done something good for them. But, with this mindset in place, so much Good-Doing is lost from the world. So, many people are not guided to a better future. Not only for themselves, but because that other individual is not allowed to arrive at a better Life-Place, then to all those that would have been helped by goodness spreading from them out to all of the rest of the world.

It seems people are always very willing to throw meanness or hurt or hate in the direction of someone who has done something or even nothing, one way or the other, to them. …Someone they do not personally know. I guess, and I have spoken about this, this is all due to the adrenalin equally euphoria that is gain by embracing that emotion of negativity. …That emotion, as negative as it is.

But, all this goes to the point of how the human race chooses to behave. At least for those who walk on the lower level of the path to consciousness. It seems, no one wants to do unless it benefits them. No one wants to do unless good has been done to and for them.

But, in living life from that level, what is made any better? Think about it, if someone is helped, then they can help. If someone is helped, they no longer have any reason to say, *"He never did anything for me."*

You can be the source of goodness spreading out to the world. All you have to do is be the impetus for that good.

Notice the need and be the one to fill that void. Help that person, whether they have ever done anything, *"Good,"* for you or not. ...Whether you know them on a personal level or not.

Be the source of doing good and the entire world becomes a better place. Because Good always spreads the Good.

* * *
06/Nov/2025 11:37 AM

How fast can you go in reverse?

WHY I DON'T LIKE PEOPLE
06/Nov/2025 09:35 AM

"Why I Don't Like People," I know the title of this piece sounds a bit harsh. And, I really don't mean it to be. But, these combined words seem kind of necessarily to spell out what I'm about to speak about.

First of all, let me ask you a question... *"Why do you go up to meet anyone?"* Now, be honest with yourself. And... *"Once you have met them, why do you continue to associate with them?"*

I'm going to let that stew with you for a little bit while a discus some of my what's what.

I'm told I tend to be a little bit standoffish. Okay, I get it. Though in casual situations I believe I am more than friendly. But, when it comes to one-on-one, I agree, I tend to stay a bit removed.

I remembered a little while back this one lady said that they had to grab me when they could because I always make an, *"Irish Exit."* Basically, for those of you like me, who may not know what that means, it is someone who leaves social gatherings without telling anyone they are leaving.

Mostly, I don't go to social gathering unless I am forced to go. And, when I do, I try to stay as removed as possible, and leave as soon as I can. Often times, without announcing the fact I am leaving. So yeah, I guess that is a true statement.

But, on a more person level, I just do not find the motivation for most people cozying up to me to be very genuine. It seems they always want something.

Just like yesterday... I was in thrift store. For those of you who know me or know about me, that's my life-distraction. It's my relax time. ...When I go out to find that treasure that I never knew existed. Like most of the time, yesterday, I found nothing. But, that's okay too... It just the visual quest.

Anyway, there is this one guy who had begun speaking to me every now and then—one of those dudes who also obviously likes the quest. So, he began a convo. No biggy. There are several people I have met that way over the years in thrift shops. All good...

He/we talked about what we talked about for a few minutes. Nothing major. Just small talk. Small talk, something I'm not good at, nor do I like. But, anyway...

It was all fine until the conversation shifted. He began to make sexual innuendos.

Now, I know this guy is married. He told me so. He even had previously showed me a photo of his wife. ...Mentioned her in the earlier part of the conversation on this day. But then, it got weird. He was subtly suggesting some really offensive sexual stuff. Finally, his last words—at least the last words I would listen to, he said, *"I'm that kind of guy."*

Wow! Okay, goodbye...

I'm not going to speculate on or about why he's married, (to a woman). But, what he was suggesting, that's just not the road I walk.

If he had been a she, I may not have been so freaked out. But...

This brings me to the point of all of this. Everybody wants something from someone. That's why they approach them in the first place. In some cases, this may be very innocent. In other cases... Well...

Like I always say, *"Everybody wants something from me, but nobody ever gives me anything."*

And, this is the case of all of life. No matter who you are, what you are, or what are the driving factors of your motivations(s), the reason people approach other people is that they want something from them.

Some people are very clear, at least in their own mind, as to what they want. Others are not that pure of heart or take the time to know themselves very well. These people are the worst offenders, as they just want. They are not even actualized enough to understand why they want it. Thus, they just go after it.

So, with all this being said, let me ask you those two original questions once again, *"Why do you go up to meet anyone?"* And... *"Once you have met them, why do you continue to associate with them?"* Mostly, *"What do you want from them."*

Be honest with yourself. You want something or you would not have made contact with them in the first place.

The world of human interaction is a strange landscape. There's a reason, there's a desire for everything. But, if you are not deeply aware of your own person motivations then what you want, from who you want it, all becomes just a process of making other people feel uncomfortable.

Be honest with yourself. Be honest with other people. Be honest from the moment you make contact. What do you want from them and why?

THE SOURCE POINT OF YOUR SPIRITUALITY
05/Nov/2025 09:29 AM

For anyone who cares about higher consciousness—spirituality by whatever definition you place on it. Or, simply wanting to be the better/best person you can be... You understand that any level of human betterment begins with yourself.

Recently, I've been spending a lot of time tracing the unfolding of how human action leads to destiny and/or the expanding reaction that surrounds a person's life based upon what they choose to do. You may have noticed this in some of my recent writings, or for those of you who attended the recent lecture series I presented.

Ultimately, and this is nothing revolutionary, and it is quite easy to trace: what you do today creates your tomorrow.

Now, this tomorrow may come at you in various fashions. It may be a direct response to what you did. Or, it may be on the much subtler level of, *"Karma,"* for lack of a better term. But, what an individual does, creates not only the next step in their world, but also directly affects those who are closely associated with them. From there, it spreads out farther and farther as each action a person takes makes other people react to and do what they do in response to that action.

As I have said forever, the one small thing that you do spreads out from you and onto the entire world. And, you can never be sure how what you do will spread out from you and onto others. ...What it will create via the next person and the next and the next that your original action impacts. Thus, you are the source of not only your universe but all of those around you from this point in time forward.

The fact is, some people set about to make what they say and what they do as large as possible. For them, the good that brings them and also the bad is the most amplified. For those who sit in silence, in mediation or simply by living their life as quietly as possible, they are the ones who cause the least amount of every-expanding chaos and thus are not the one who encounter the greater reaping of reactions based upon what they have done.

Do you ever think about this? Do you ever question how your actions will affect others? And, what will be the consequences of your actions on your life as they will ultimately lead back to you?

The fact of the fact is, and I say this all the time, most people do not live their life from the position of consciousness. They just do what makes them feel good or at least better. They live their life not defined by a deeper truth but simply by whatever opinion it is that they hold in whatever given moment.

But, what occurs from this? Answer: chaos and negative karma.

As those of you who have read this blog over the past decade or so understand, and for those of you who have read my other writings know, I often discuss my personal experiences and what they mean to not only me but the greater reality in general. I do this because I believe that living life, and living it consciously, is the ultimate teacher for walking the spiritual path and diving deeper into the true understanding of higher consciousness. Because it is only from within you that you may find that deeper understanding that is true to your heart.

Let me say that no matter what you do or do not believe in, no matter what greater truth you seek, if you seek any at all, what you do and how you live your life—and, how you react to what is done to you, comes to be not only your best and most truthful teacher but the source point for the all of the spiritually that will or will not define your life. What you do in each life situation not only sets your next level of experiences into motion, but what you do will spread out from you creating an untold number of life events in the lives or all those who are impacted by the wave you created with your initial action. …People that you will never know.

Thus, I can say, always do what you do with a refined sense of consciousness. Try very hard to only do helpful and good things. And, always be kind.

All those who walk a higher path say similar things. Nothing new here. But, as we are all surrounded by a world driven by people who are only guided by random emotions and a need to fulfill whatever desire it is that they hold, what must become your focus, if you truly hope to live a better life, defined by a higher purpose, you must focus upon how you create what you create, not only defined by what you do but by what is done to you.

Take your life experiences and learn from them. Be honest with yourself. Very consciously watch what you do and how you react to what is done to you. Take control. Only allow the good to spread from you. For it is only you who can do it.

THE BAD THINGS THAT YOU DO
03/Nov/2025 04:32 PM

I went to the supermarket this afternoon to pick up some stuff for lunch and for dinner. To give you a little bit of a back story, I've been going to that supermarket for well over twenty years.

As I was pulling into this parking spot—a parking spot I have pulled into an uncountable number of times before, this flashback came to my mind. It was a time, maybe twenty years deep and I was going to that supermarket in the early afternoon. It was a cloudy day in SoCal, I remember that. And, I pulled into the parking spot with little thought. I then went into the supermarket, also with little thought. As I was returning to my car, I saw this elderly gentleman shoving a shopping cart into the front fender of my car. I, of course, speeded up my pace, with my groceries in hand, yelling *"Hey!"* I approached the man, asking him why did he smack the shopping cart into my car? He, of course, denied the fact. He said it was already there, and he was just pulling it loose from my car. Liar!

Looking at my car, which was at that time a 2002 Honda Civic, I noticed that a rather large crease had been shoved into my front left fender, in the area just above the front tire.

This was pretty upsetting. I certainly wasn't wealthy at that time, meaning it wasn't something that I could just easily go and quickly have repaired. And, it's one of those things that you can't really report to the insurance company or they're going to raise your rates.

But, that's not really the point to all of this; is it? I asked the man, why did he do it? He kept denying that he did. I looked at him, very deeply in the eyes, just to let him know that I knew the truth. But again, what could I do?

Sure, I could have kicked his ass. That would have been pretty easy to do. But then I would have probably ended up in jail. I could have yelled and screamed at him. But, what would that prove? It wouldn't change what he did—it wouldn't change his life and make him become a better person. I could have called the cops. But, he would have just deny what he did to them as he did to me. Thus, all of what I could dos would have solved nothing. Me, I was left with a dent in the left front fender of my car.

Like I say, I was kind of going through a poor stretch back then, and I didn't really have the money to immediately get it fixed. Every time I saw it, however, it really upset me. I really wanted to get it repaired to just forget about the incident.

Finally, when I got a royalty check from one of my publishers, and this was about three months later, I was able to pay to have my car fixed. I took it to one of those paintless dent removal places, and they removed the dent very nicely, I must say. It cost me about three hundred bucks to get it done.

But, to the point of all of this… There I was, having to deal with something bad that someone else had done. …Done to me. …And, what did that doing really prove but to mess up my life?

Maybe that's what that guy wanted to do??? I don't know? He didn't know me. I didn't know him. But, he just wanted to fuck with somebody. Why? Who knows? I guess just because he was existing in the space of the Really Small Mind. …Desiring to hurt someone else/anyone else for whatever he had lived through/whatever had been done to him/whatever he was feeling—feeling for whatever reason, and this was his only resolve to that emotion, to hurt the life of someone else.

I imagine we've all gone through somewhat of a similar circumstance. Someone hurt us for no good goddamn reason. I mean, hopefully you haven't… But, most of us probably have experienced something like this, to some degree or another.

I believe all of this takes us to the level of deeper thought. A place where we really need to question the reality that we live in, and the reality that we project.

I mean, really think about this… Let's take this away from the victim mentality and take it to the perpetrator mentality. Think about your own life. Who have you hurt? Did you hurt them intentionally like this guy did to me? If you did, why did you do it? Did you do it so they would feel the pain you feel? Did you do it because you felt you had the right to do it? Did you do it because you felt you could get away with it? Did you do it because you felt they deserved it? Or, did you do it for no specific reason?

A lot of people in this world, I would guess probably most, live in a space of Unrefined Consciousness. Meaning, they do what they do without really giving it any thought. They just act. They just react. …Driven by whatever emotion and/or whatever unresolved feelings that they may possess.

How does that pertain to you? Do you behave in this manner?

Again, let's go back to the question, whom have you hurt and why have you hurt them? And, if you have hurt them, have you ever gone back and repaired the damage that you created? Did you ever repair the dent in their left front fender of their car?

I believe that some low-minded people actually get lost in the fact that they have the right to do whatever they want to do, say whatever they want to say, and hurt whomever they want or hurt. Sure, there's Free Speech and all of that kind of stuff in places like the United States. Sure, some people are bad-assed brawlers. But, words equal actions, equal pain. And, if you have caused someone pain, what do you think that that has done to your life? Did you ever look at what happened to your life <u>next</u> after you did something that hurt someone else? Did you ever study the repercussions that you may have experienced? And, if you didn't, what does that say about the higher state of your mental being? Doesn't it mean you just don't give a fuck? And if you don't give a fuck, what does that say about your true human nature?

Like I say, we probably all have experienced something like what I am speaking about. …The attack unleashed by some other person throughout the progression of our lives.

At best, all we can do is deal with the repercussions as best as we can deal with them. Save up the money, and eventually get the fender fixed.

But, all of this comes down to the deeper level of YOU. Because YOU are the ultimate causation factor in the All and the Everything. It's you who has the ability to smash that shopping cart into somebody's left front fender. It's also you, no matter what your anger level is, no matter what your level of frustration is, no matter what has happened to you in the past, no matter whatever exists in the all of your everything of your life, it is YOU who has the ability to make the choice to never hurt anyone.

The person who never hurts anyone is the greatest person that can exist.

So, who do you want to be? How do you want to be defined and remembered? As someone who has hurt someone? Or, as a person who is thought of as someone who always helped everybody and never hurt anyone? And, if you did hurt anyone, you repaired all the damaged you created?

Your life, your choice.

As for me, I never saw that guy again. What happened to him, who knows? I've parked in that parking spot so many times, I can't even remember how many. I've lived in this neighborhood a long, long time. But, just like today, what that guy did to me will always be in my mind. I may not be thinking about it all the time, but every now and then, when I pull into that parking space, that bad deed will come to mind. And, it will make me question why some people do what they do. Why do some people do what they do?

My advice, hurt no one. Then, not only does the life of everyone else, but your own life, become a much better place.

TELL ME A LITTLE BIT ABOUT YOURSELF
02/Nov/2025 05:55 AM

"Tell me a little bit about yourself?"
"What do you do for a living?"
"What do you believe in?"
"What do you do for fun?"

How you define yourself, not only to others around you in the world, but especially to yourself, comes to be the projected definition of your life.

Now certainly, this seems like a very obvious statement. But, if you move this towards a little bit deeper level, and really think this through, *"How do you define yourself?"* Truly! And, *"How do you define yourself to others?"* Truly!

I had to do this little session in the Midwest last week. In the AM of one of the days that I was there, I decided to pop into a *Panera* and have one of their Avo and Egg White Breakfast Sandwiches and a cup of their tasty Hazelnut Coffee for breakfast. I grabbed my stuff and went and sat down at a table.

I noticed there was an older guy working on his computer, at the booth behind me, and a middle-aged lady sitting a table, also behind me. No biggy. But, you always need to be aware of your surroundings.

I sat down and began to eat my breakfast sandwich. I hear the lady begin to talk. I initially assumed she was on her phone, as I could not see her—as she was behind me. She went into what sounded like a discourse. She began to go on and on and on about how she had been sexually attacked. Then, she went deeper into the subject. It was by her husband, which had caused her to have extensive anxiety.

The conversation, or whatever it was, was very intense. She gave this entire definition of her life and what brought her to the point where she found herself.

Maybe not convo, I thought? Maybe she was writing a book or preparing a lecture, as there did not seem to be a response or a back and forth in any manner.

What she spoke, she said in a very articulate manner.

Finally, it was over, and there, again, was the silence you expect in such an establishment.

I finished up my breakfast. Was enjoying my cup of coffee. And, was doing some doomscrolling on my phone.

Then, she went into it again. Another conversation??? This time, she began to detail how she had been sexually assaulted which caused her to leave her relationship. But, as she had developed a certain sense and stye of living, her former mate had, *"The responsibility,"* as she put it, to keep her living at that level. So, she was getting alimony—getting money from him and she deserved it!

…This made think to my former brother-in-law who is getting palimony from his ex, my sister-in-law. What a loser! Be a man!

But, that's a side note, never mind…

Again, she went on and on and on. Speaking of sexual abuse, anxiety, all the pain, psychological and otherwise was in, getting money for free, and how she deserved it. But, all her friends had taken the side of her ex-husband and would not speak to her, so she was all alone.

The definition of her life. She really had it all down pat.

Finally, I couldn't take anymore. I got up and looked to my rear. The older guy had already taken off and moved to a different table in the distance to get whatever work done that he needed completed on his laptop. I look, the lady had not been on her phone or her tape recorder or her anything as I had thought. She was just speaking to herself. And, I guess anyone who would listen. Wow!

Me, I put my plate on the used plate area. Grabbed another cup of the joe for the road. And, I was out-a-there.

Now, this is a very extreme sense of a person possessing a highly defined definition of themselves and their life and their... And, wanting to get it out there to the world. ...As negative as all of that was... But, we all hold a definition of our life.

I believe what comes to be the question of this definition, however, is how true is this characterization? How honest are you with yourself? And, how much do you project that definition to the world? How much do you want others to truly know about you?

I mean, on the very minuet level, think of all the people who wear tee-shirts featuring a band that they like or a jersey from the sports team they follow. That is a definition of who they are. It spreads out from there. What you wear is assuredly a definition of who you are and how you see yourself. But, more importantly, what you say and particularly what you do comes to be the ideal projection of who you think you are.

So truly, who are you? And, how much time have you spent truly defining who and what you actually are? Mostly, is who you think you are, truly who and what you actually are? Or, are you lying to yourself and the world around you?

Perhaps, even equally important, how do you project your self-definition out to the world? Is how you view yourself—is how you define yourself—is how you project yourself based in a mind frame of positivity or is it based in the ideology of negativity? Do you define yourself by the positive events in your life or the negative events that you have undergone? Knowing, that by embracing the positive you are viewed by others in one way, and that ways sets the course for your new and next set of life adventures, verse using negativity as a self-definition.

The world begins with you. Your world begins with you. How you define yourself, how you project yourself, will forever lay the foundations for your next set of life experiences.

* * *
02/Nov/2025 05:10 AM

The last person that you said anything negative about will become the definition of your life.

* * *
02/Nov/2025 05:10 AM

If you take anything from someone else to make your living, you will forever be in debt.

* * *
01/Nov/2025 07:21 AM

You can't realize you need to stop doing something until you start doing something.

*   *   *
01/Nov/2025 07:19 AM

Bumping into someone once is an accident.

Bumping into someone twice is a coincidence.

Bumping into someone three times is stalking.

FUN IN THE SUN
26/Oct/2025 01:49 PM

The new Prime Minster of Japan is a female. Previously, she was a drummer in a Heavy Metal Band. You gotta kind of love that.

Apparently, from what I've heard on the news, she is very conservative and highly anti-immigration.

I don't know if you pay attention to such stuff, but Japan has been overrun with tourism since the end of the pandemic. Why? I don't really know. But, it seems that everyone is going there. Even a lot of people I have come into contact with. ...Going for the first time. And, I get it, Japan is a great and very beautiful country. I have spent a large portion of my adult life retuning to Japan. ...I've spent a lot of time there. In fact, I had the plan to make it my homebase forever. But, that did not work out. At least not yet.

Now, when I go there, I too see the overwhelming nature of tourists. For example, my lady is really into Hello Kitty. Because of this fact, we periodically go to Sanrio Puroland. When we went just before the pandemic, we were the only non-Japanese people there. The last time we went, a couple of months ago, it was overwhelmed by non-Japanese. It was crazy!

One funny thing that happened while we were there was this one very large and overweight female American of Hispanic descent was there with her teenage daughter. You could tell, the mother was way into Hello Kitty. But, you know how teenagers are, anything your parents are into, you probably hate. The daughter was obviously not into it. The mother, almost yelling at her, *"You will have fun here!"* Kind of like a drill sergeant. To witness it, it was pretty funny…

The thing is, there has been talk of this advanced rate of tourism in Japan for a while now. They even started charging a travel fee for foreigners to enter the country last month, (I think it was). When you think of this kind of stuff, you, (meaning me), always imagine it's the Americans causing the problem. But, as it turns out, that is not wholly true. Well, they are, at least in part. But, it is actually, and more so, the Chinese that are the big issue of tourism in Japan.

Like, I was walking in this park in Osaka, the last time I was there, and surrounding me, literally everywhere, were people of Chinese origin sitting and picnicking, and all of that kind of stuff. To the average Westerner, they might not even notice the difference, as the Chinese are also Asian. But, to the Japanese, there is a very big difference.

I think to Hong Kong. It's really a sight. Every Sunday, swarms of all of the Filipinos and Filipinas, who work in Hong Kong, congregate in Central, grab a spot on the ground, hang out, talk, eat, dance, sing, you name it. It's really very cool. At least I think so. But, I too am not a Hong Kong National. So, how do the true locals feel about this?

By nature, the Japanese have always been understood to be an ethnocentric race. Just look to the annals of history to confirm this fact. And, this is not a criticism or an insult in any way. So, I get it, too many foreigners are coming in and probably overstaying their tourist visa and all of that kind of stuff and messing with their culture and the country. I know that's big problem here in the States, as well. That too has been all over the news, with President Trump instigating a major crackdown.

It was kind of interesting, I thought… Here in the L.A. area, there had long been a certain amount of tourism from China. You would see the tourist buses delivering the crew and the like. Then came the pandemic, and China went into a major lockdown. A lockdown that lasted longer than much of the rest of the world. Once that finally broke open, there was a noticeable deluge of people speaking Mandarin and other China-based dialects all over the place here in the great Los Angeles region. It was and is a noticeable tidal wave.

But, what does all this mean? What does it mean to Japan? What does it mean to the world society as a whole? And, what does it mean that the people in power wish to stop the flow of various groups of people crossing a country's boarders?

I mean, I too am a fault. Like I say, I've spent a lot of my Life Time in Japan. I wish I could have spent more. Back in the 1980s and into the '90s, a white guy with long blonde hair was seen as cool and a welcomed traveler, promising promises. Now??? It seems there has been a shift in the way outsiders are viewed.

There has always been this sentiment in the States, as well. It happened with all of the various new introduction of ethnic groups and races that came here. And certainly, this is nothing limited to Japan or the States. It has gone on across the world forever. There is racism everywhere. I, most certainly, have experienced it.

Like I have long understood, eventually, if humanity lasts that long, there will only be one race. But, until then, there will undoubtedly always be discrimination due to race—particularly a person's race in another land.

The thing is, it is a very low level of consciousness to judge a person by their race or their ethnic or cultural origin. But, it goes on all the time. Listen and you will hear, *"That person is a Jew, a Muslim, a Christian, a Black, a White,"* and all of the much more derogatory terms that are used to define the various groups and races. But, should that be the end-all definition of a person? Where they come from or the color of their skin?

Certainly, I'm not saying anything new here. It has all been said before. But, what all this drives us to is the question, who are you? How do you define another person? Do you define them by where they come from and not what they do, how they treat other people, and/or the good that they give verses the bad that they unleash?

Think of any place/any country in the world. How many people in that country do good things verses how many of them do bad things. Now, take this down to the more personal level, how does that one specific individual, from that different far-off place, treat you and treat others? Do they do good things for you? Or, do they do bad things?

Let's take this one step deeper... How do you behave? How do you behave when you are in your home country, your home city, in your home? And, perhaps even more importantly—at least in terms of this discussion, how do you behave when you are somewhere else? Do you respect the culture and contribute only good to it? Or, do you hold onto your customs and do things that might be found offensive by the traditions and understandings of this Other Place?

Like I always say, the entire world begins with you. It begins with what you think, what you say, and what you do. What you do spreads out from you and onto the All and the Everything. Thus, what you do causes others to judge not only you but your entire culture. Again, what do you do?

Most people never think of this. Most people never think about anyone but themselves. They do not care what impact they may have on anyone or anything else, as long as they are okay. But, is that the way anyone should behave? Is that the impact you wish to feel by someone from some far-off land?

Near or far, people are people. What you do sets an entire chain reaction into motion everywhere around you. This chain reaction may be small, it may be large. It may be helpful, or it may be hurtful. It may cause others to love or to hate you and your peoples.

Ultimately, all you can do/all you should do is to be respectful of all human life and never do anything that changes the natural order of things. In fact, you should never do anything that breaks the flow of a culture or a tradition or even a single person. Because, when that occurs, all that it does is make you the source point for a lot of negative karma which can branch out from you and affect the greater world as a whole. Do you wish to be sourcepoint for that?

Think before you do.

WARDROBE CHECK
24/Oct/2025 01:16 PM

As I say way too often, there is rarely a week that goes by that I do not receive some question about, *The Roller Blade Seven*. Mostly, I just kind of let most of them go in one ear and out the other—because they always seem to be the same question(s), asked and answered so many times before. People, just don't want to do their research. But, that's life...

Sometimes, if the question strikes a point of interest in me, I will answer it directly. Other questions, I feel are best answered in places like this—this blog, so that more people who have wondered can read the reveal. That's like this question I received the other day...

I'm sure I've spoken about this (somewhere) before, but I can't place where or when. So, I will address it here.

I was asked about my wardrobe for *The Roller Blade Seven*. Where did the idea for my costuming come from and who supplied it.

To answer:

Basically, it was just the style of clothing I have worn forever. I have long worn suits and/or sport coats and slacks. Plus, I (virtually) always wear tennis shoes. So, when it came time to dress my character, Hawk, for the film, that's just the direction I decided to go towards. Don was fine with it.

The suit I wore, of which there were actually two, was a black Armani. I already owned one of them, and I picked up another one shortly after we went into production. So, one could be being dry cleaned and I would have a backup. The black shirt or shirts that I wore were made my Ralph Lauren, of which I had five. The shoes I wore we mid-high tops made by Reebok, of which I added purple shoelaces. I had two pairs.

Interesting note: The Art Director on the shoot hated the fact that I put purple shoelaces in the shoes. Why? I really don't know??? But, he made several comments about how I needed to remove them and replace them with traditional laces. But, this film was Don and my baby, so I just disregarded everything/anything he said.

The skates I wore were made by Rollerblade. I forget what actual model they were, but I'm sure there are you Rollerblade experts out there who would know, as they were very distinctive with the dayglow green wheels and upper strap, with dayglow blue accents.

I bought those skates just before we went into production at a sporting goods store at the Beverly Connection shopping center. A sweet lady friend of mine, Laurie, and I went over there, after Don and I had been in preproduction all day, as the first shoot date was quickly approaching. I remember they cost me about a hundred and fifty bucks.

The knee pads, elbow pads, and hand pads were something I picked up at the same time. I knew I was not a good skater and I really wanted to protect myself as much as I could as I had no illusion about the fact that I was probably going to hit the ground more than once.

In terms of the Rollerblades, as stated, I was/am not much of a skater, so it ended up that I rarely wore them in the film. You can see a few fun (not really) adventures of me wearing them in *The Roller Blade Seven* Documentary I made, *Roller Blade Seven: The Unseen Scenes* on YouTube.

Now, let me address the red sock. It's a subtle thing, but if you look closely at the film, and listen to the subtle dialogue, both Don and my character wear one red sock all the time. And, characters like the one played by Allison, wear one red legging.

In fact, Don had one seat in his 1962 Plymouth Belvedere upholstered red and one of the front rims on the car painted red.

What does it mean??? Shuuu… That's a secret. I can't tell you. No, not really.

It was just a sublet reference point designed to signify that only a small group of the characters were a true part of the Cult that was *The Roller Blade Seven.*

It always surprises me that so many people have seen this film, and so many people have talked shit about it, but they have never taken the time to actually study the sublet elements and reality of the film. And yes, there is A LOT of subtle messaging in the movie. Messages that those who go into, thinking that they already know what they know, completely miss.

I guess that's the true essence of Art, Artistic Cinema, and *Zen Filmmaking,* it's so sublet you have to understand Art before you can truly witness and become a part of the Art.

Anyway… I'm sure there is a million other things I could say about this subject, but that's pretty much the All and Everything on my wardrobe.

THE LIES IN THE TRUTH
21/Oct/2025 07:27 AM

Have you ever worked for and received a degree or a certification or a something in a something, or maybe you did something that not too many other people have accomplished? Then, when it was mentioned that you had achieved that something-something, did someone else claimed that you did not do it? They had no proof of this fact. They were just believing whatever it is they were believing; based upon whatever false reality they were living in. Nonetheless, their claiming it caused doubt about who you are, what you've done, what you've achieved, and what you may have accomplished.

I always find the reality of this reality interesting. There is so much truth out there based upon so many lies. Yes, a lot of people do claim things that are just not true. And, in this day and age there's ways to fabricate an entire existence. But, what is a lie? A lie is only a lie. This being said, there is a whole other reality. There are people that actually work to achieve something. They go through the process. They take the courses. They take the tests. And, they gain the degrees or the certifications or the whatever.

There are also those who go out and actually do that something-something that few other people have done. The list of these accomplishments and/or certifications are vast. So, there's no real way to limit them to just one or two things. This being said, it seems that for everything someone achieves, there is always someone who claims that what they are saying is a lie.

Look around the Internet. So many people are saying so many negative things about so many people. It's really sad.

But, disparaging someone does not change the truth of their truth.

I think back to a funny situation that happened to me in Bangkok, Thailand in the later part of the 1980s. After the point I earned my Ph.D., I was sometimes using the title doctor in front of my name instead of mister. You know, I thought it may get me better service and the like… Yeah, I was a bit young, I guess??? I was twenty-eight when I earned the degree and I was probably thirty when this situation I'm about to explain took place. But, that's really not all that young considering there are a lot of academics out there now who have earned their doctorate at the age of twenty-one. No comparison intended, but Albert Einstein earned his at the age of twenty-six. So…

But, that was then, this is now. …Now, when asked I about it, I just say, *"It has expired…"* Like I used to use as my bio-line, *"Former Swami, Former Punk Rocker, Former Ph.D."*

Back to the story before I get too far off track… I was having lunch at the coffee shop of the Oriental Hotel along the Chao Praya River in Bangkok. Thai people are not noted for being subtle in any manner. That's not an insult; that's just a statement, based in the reality of their cultural norm. In fact, they can be quite straightforward in what may be considered as quite rude by other cultures. Anyway, I was sitting there enjoying my lunch when I hear this one of the staff members, a waiter, just ripping me up and down. It was really quite funny because he didn't realize that I could understand Thai. He was saying all of these really negative comments about me. Saying I could not be a doctor? I was way too young. I had long hair. And, just going on and on and on and on to whoever would listen.

When he came back to my table, to ask if I had enjoyed my meal, I decided to speak to him in Thai. I told him thanks for the meal, and could I have my check. Obviously, he was quite taken aback by me speaking Thai. Me, however, I thought it all was very-very funny, as I'm not one of those people who has ego riding on any of that kind of stuff. …Or, gets insulted by that kind of nonsense.

In any case, he went all into apology mode and all of that kind of stuff. All the kind of stuff I really didn't care about or need to hear.

See, this is just one of the facts of the facts of life, people believe what they want to believe. But, much of what they believe is based upon nothing more than their own internal projection. And, some people are very loud in their beliefs, as wrong as those beliefs may be. Have you ever had anything like that happen to you? Have you ever done anything like that?

I know in the martial arts, that kind of nonsense has gone on forever. Everybody has insulted the rank of other people, questioning and claiming it was not real. Or, somebody earned it in some fake way. Or, proclaiming that person is just No Good and they are better. Yet, the people who are proclaiming all that kind of stuff, based upon negativity, it always seems to turn out that they are the false practitioners who are not grounded in any true sense of the martial arts. And, not only do they not possess advanced rank themselves, but they are really walking a very dark road because they are not embracing the true essence of the martial arts which is self and generalized positivity.

The point I'm trying to make here is, life is based upon what you believe. That's the case for everyone. But, if what you believe is not based in the truth, but is instead based upon the not-true, what are you left with? And, if what you believe is based upon the false projection of someone else. …Somebody else who believes they are the one who possesses the capacity to define another individual, yet, they are wrong, then what? What is the truth of the lie you believe?

I think it's important for you to take a look at your own life. What have you believed? What have you told others you believe? Where did you gain the beliefs that you hold? And, have you ever been real enough with yourself, when you find out that you are wrong, to truly correct not only what you believed, but what you projected about that other individual or that other situation to others? Have you ever owned your lie? Have you ever owned your false, judgmental-based projections?

If you look at people, you find that many/most of them are based in ego. Ego, meaning that they do everything from a position of Self. What does operating from a position of Self actually mean? It means that they are selfish. They are only thinking about themselves. They are only seeing reality as they choose to see it. Whether that reality be true or false.

By behaving in this manner, all of life—the life of that person and the lives of all the people that person influences are altered for the negative. Why? Because they are solely operating from the very limited perception of what they want and/or choose to believe. But, belief is not necessarily the truth.

Think about this as you go through life. Think about this as you believe what you believe. Think about this as you listen to what other people believe. Is what they're saying based in fact? Or, is what they're saying simply based in what they're projecting onto the reality of this place we call Life?

You can help or hurt this reality. Your life. Your choice.

* * *
20/Oct/2025 12:24 PM

Is your life defined by what you have achieved or by what you have not achieved?

CULTURAL APPROPRIATION
20/Oct/2025 08:17 AM

I went to the Diwali festival the other evening...

Let me go Side Bar here on you for a second—just to give you the what's what. Diwali, or more properly Dipavali, is the Hindu Festival of Lights. It symbolizes the victory of light over darkness.

Anyway, there were thousands of people. And, when I say thousands, I truly mean thousands at the temple. Most, were of South Asian descent. They came as this is one of their high holidays.
Everything was great. It was a beautiful event. The temple was lighted with all of these colorful lights, and the people were all truly enjoying themselves, while basking in the holiness of this holy day.
I wasn't the only person of non-South Asian descent there, however. There were a few other Caucasians, and Asians from various other regions of the globe. The one thing that I took note of, however, and the thing that kind of gave me pause, was that I did notice a number of Westerners wearing South Asian garb. Meaning, they were dressed in clothing most commonly associated with India.
The thing that kind of made me think, and the things that that gave me pause, was the fact that these people were all behaving in a very, (let me say), disrespectful manner; laughing and joking in the Mandir and the like.
They didn't really get it! They were there, they knew this event was going on, but they weren't there for the right reasons. Plus, they were doing what is most commonly associated with cultural appropriation. They were dressing in a garb from a different land and a different tradition, but they didn't even understand the root of the culture.

The thing is, every style of South Asian clothing is worn by a very specific religious sect. Meaning, one type of person who follows the Hindu religion may wear a very different style of clothing than another person who follows the Hindu religion.

Now, this is all fine. You see the various styles of clothing, worn by the different people, and it is all very natural. But, these are people that were born into that tradition. They are not people that are putting on a costume and pretending. They live it. The Westerners do not.

I don't know, I find all of that a bit offensive.

Certainly, one could have said the same thing about me in my younger years. But, the difference between me and these other Westerners, is that I was actually living the Hindu lifestyle. I was a yogi.

I've told this story before, but I think it's very definitive of the difference between someone who dresses up to play a role and someone who is actually living what they are living.

As the story goes, I was walking over to the local supermarket, to pick up something for Sister Maji, who was the main chef at the Los Angeles Integral Yoga Institute. I was sixteen or seventeen years old. Anyway, I stood there on Sunset Blvd., about to walk across the street, and some young girls drove up to the stoplight. I believe they had Iowa plates on their car. With their window down, they looked at me, and they asked, *"Are you a hippie?"* My immediate answer was, *"No, I'm a yogi."* The light turned green, and I walked across the street.

After I had got what I got at the supermarket, I went back to the IYI, and I told Sister Maji about the story. She said, *"You see Shiva Das, God was testing you."* I guess I passed.

What I will say is that, I believe, playing dress up is really disrespectful of other people's culture, unless, like I was, you're living it.

Sure, if it was for a movie, or something like that, I get it. But, to just do it to do it, and not even understand what you're wearing, why you're wearing it, what you're wearing it means, or why you're even doing any of what you're doing really robs the entire energy of any situation. Don't you think?

I suppose you could say that cultural appropriation goes on all over the place. I mean, Hinduism was born in India. The Buddha was a Hindu. The religion that was founded around his teachings occurred in India, traveled to China, where it was embraced to a certain degree. But, then it found its true home in Japan, where it flourished. So, people took something, and absorbed it, born in a different land, created by an entirely different culture. Yet, it became what it was to become in a completely separate land.

The difference that I believe took place is that the culture of Japan took the understanding of the religion, but made it their own. They lived it! They were not pretending to be something they were not.

So, all of this is just something to think about. Ask yourself, do you play dress up, do you pretend to be something you're not, simply defined by the clothing you're wearing? Or, do you truly live who you truly are, defined by everything you think, what you do, how you do it, and the all and the everything else?

In other words, are you real or are you a fake?

*   *   *

16/Oct/2025 12:58 PM

The good news is, more than likely you are probably not going to remember this moment.

The bad news is, more than likely you are probably not going to remember this moment.

THE LIGHT THAT NEVER TURNS ON
16/Oct/2025 08:32 AM

I have this Arri Fresnel mounted on top of my bookshelf. It has sat up there for a lot of years—mounted on one of those bolt-on clamps. I used to have it plugged in, thinking I would use it. But, I never did. So, I unplugged it way back in the way back when.

I have this other Fresnel, a DeSisti, sitting over in one corner. I put it there... ...Wow, way back when. I thought it would be a good idea to keep it there just in case I needed it in a pinch. Have never used it. At least not so far...

My storage unit... Forget about it. I've got tons of lights and stands.

One upon a time, in the long ago and the far-far away, I used to have to load up all those lights and drag them along whenever I was doing a shoot. You know, all to give the production a vibe. I was all into the highly gelled looked. That was my method to get it.

Somewhere in my filmmaking evolution, however, I stopped doing all of that. I got, for lack of a better term, Natural.

Back when I was teaching a lot of classes and seminars on filmmaking... (Before the pandemic and before classes got all remote. I just don't like teaching in that manner). I would do this one thing in order to teach the students how quickly you can change the entire vibe of a scene simply by doing one small thing.

I would set up the camera and feed it into the monitor. I would have all the lights on in a classroom; as is commonly the case. I would focus on the face of one of my students. Then, I would have another one of the students turn off half of the lights in the classroom. BAM, instantly everything changed. The entire way you look at what is being filmed on the screen is altered.

Like I have long discussed, and taught, any filmmaker, any cinematographer really needs to learn to see what the camera sees; not just what the human eye sees; as from this, you can make the photography of your film great or very bland.

But, like I said, somewhere along the way, I begin to leave the lights behind. Now, I shoot au naturel.

That's not to say that someday, the inspiration will not strike, and I will take it all back to the way back when. But, as my *Zen Filmmaking* style has evolved, and I have moved to the *Non-Narrative Zen Film,* it has simply become my method.

But, the fact of the fact is, how you find yourself in any situation is defined by the light that surrounds you or the light you create. You can bring in the lighting fixtures. You can focus them. You can gel them up. You can place them to totally create the lighting definition that you desire. …Making a scene look any way that you want. Or, you can simply let the light be as it—as you found it.

Which is best? I don't know, what do you think?

Life is either allowed to be as life is. Or, you can attempt to control it. If you let it be as it is, you are free. All you have to do is to live and capture that moment. Or, you can try to dominate it. Then, the all and the everything gets way more complicated.

Your life, your choice.

THE PLAYER IN THE PLAYER
15/Oct/2025 02:40 PM

Regarding the world of AI and the supreme knowledge of the Being AI. And yes, AI is a Being—an Entity onto itself. …It has, like for many of us, continued to amaze me.

Well… Amazement may not be the right word. But, it certainly has continued to interest me and to cause me to question the reality of reality.

So, much of it is right. Yet, so much of it is wrong.

The thing that I find the most curious—telling is that you ask the same question five times and you will, (most commonly), get five different answers.

I can say, I sure wish it was around when I was in school. Damn, it would have made the process so much easier!

Anyway… I'm not really one of those people who searches myself on the internet. It's just not who I am. Nor am I all that interested in what other people have to say about me. Because mostly, all that is being voiced is by people who have never met me and most of what I have found that they are saying is wrong.

But today, a university student, who wrote a paper on *Zen Filmmaking* and Yours Truly, sent me a copy of it. I found it kinda interest—kinda funny. *"Thanks,"* I guess…

In it, he quotes a few things that he got from the World of Google AI Mode about me. At one point, I guess he searched me in association with the Robert Altman film, *The Player,* where I briefly appear.

I'm quoting the quote,

"In Robert Altman's 1992 film, The Player, the actor Scott Shaw has an uncredited cameo role, playing himself. The primary scene he appeared in was deleted from the Final Cut of the film.

Film: The Player (1992).
Director: Robert Altman.
Role: An uncredited cameo as himself. One of many real-life celebrities who made a brief appearance in the film to lampoon the Hollywood system.
Context: Shaw was personally asked by Altman to appear in the film.

Details of the deleted scene: The scene was shot at the Beverly Hills Hotel and involved Shaw being interviewed by an aggressive reporter. The deleted scene features Shaw, in character as himself. During the conversation, a discussion ensues about the use of martial arts in films. Shaw gives his perspective on the differences between Eastern martial arts and what Hollywood uses in movies.

Shaw explained that the scene was improvised and described the improvised dialogue as "priceless." However, in an archival interview about the production with Altman, the director explained that several scenes, including Shaw's, were cut to reduce the film's runtime.

Final product: While Shaw's scene and many others were ultimately cut, the intent was to build a rich tapestry of the film's Hollywood setting by including as many real industry figures as possible.

It is common for celebrity cameos to be left on the cutting room floor, especially in a film like The Player, which featured a huge number of well-known personalities. The removal of these cameos was not unusual for The Player. A large number of celebrity appearances were filmed, but many ended up on the cutting room floor as Altman and his editors shaped the final story. Other deleted scene include a scene with Jeff Daniels playing golf and Patrick Swayze showing off his karate moves."

Though this all makes for an interesting read... I guess??? It does not mention the one scene I shot that did make it into the final cut of film, where I'm watching the movie, The Bicycle Thief in the theatre and Tim Robbins, the lead character, comes up to me after the film, as I am walking up the stairs, and confuses me with the guy his character eventually kills. So much for AI.

So yes, the scene that is being discussed was cut. But yes, I still am in the film.

Anyway, just some food for thought.

Life is funny don't you think? There is all that stuff that you live, but no one else really experienced it because they weren't there. They can research it. They can AI it. They can write and talk about it. But, no one but you knows what really went on and what it was like to live it.

GLAD I COULD BE OF HELP
14/Oct/2025 02:04 PM

    I was just speaking about people that end up living on the fringes of society, in the previous blog, and how you should protect yourself from ending up in such a situation. So, I thought it was karmically interesting when I bumped into this one lady I have observed this AM.

    I may have mentioned her in the past. But, I've seen her around for a year or so. She normally hangs out in this one parking lot I frequent, as it is tied to this Starbucks I go to several days of the week. Anyway, she walks around asking people for money. Okay...

    She's of Indian descent. One day I asked her, and she said she was originally from New Delhi. Like I told her, me, I've spent a certain about of time there...

    Anyway, she's a curious persons, at least in my mind. I mean, what's her backstory? I always feel uncomfortable saying this but where I live is considered an affluent neighborhood. And, she's around everyday; begging... Not like a monk would do. More like a homeless person. She's a fixture. I see her a lot and I've spoken with her from time to time.

    The thing is, she lives in this neighborhood. I discovered that the other day when I saw her, and the son she has spoken about, going into this one residence. If you live here, why beg? I mean how can you afford to live in this neighborhood via begging?

    It was a rainy day today, and I was going into my local CVS. For those of you who may not know, or for the annals of history, CVS is a drug store. There she was standing under the awning, out in front. She tried to sell me a hat she had in a bag. *"No thanks. I don't carry any cash."* *"Can you help me out with some food?"* *"Sure. What do you want?"* *"Anything cheap. Like something from the bagel store."* *"Of course!"*

As we walked over to the nearby bagel shop, I asked her about her husband. She told me that he will not help her. That she must take care of herself. She must find her own way to eat. Wow!

I asked if he was also from India. She said he was. *"Oh, I see."* She knew that I knew.

Here's the thing. And, this is a thing that is not right. Nor is it conscionable. Nor am I being ethnocentric, racist, or anything like that here. But, in India, people are forced into marriages. I won't go into all of that. But, as is well documented, many/most marriages are arranged. And sometimes, the couple is just not well suited. Nor, as is apparently the case with this woman, is her man a true man. From this, sometimes things can get messy.

Now, here's the thing. I don't know the deep truth about this woman, her son, her husband, or her situation. In fact, I don't want to know. I avoid messy lives at all costs. I don't want to get sucked in to anything negative. But, what I was happy to do, was to be able to buy her something to eat. Because, if she had food at home, I can't imagine she would be out in the rain begging for money or food.

In the bagel shop, one that I used to grab bagels from quite frequently, pre-pandemic, I asked her what she wanted. *"Anything you want."* She was very adamant with the young man at the counter that it could have no meat. I mean, sure, she's a Hindu, so a vegetarian. She decided on an avocado bagel sandwich type thing. I whipped out my phone. Paid. And I was out of there. *"Good luck,"* I exclaimed. *"Happy Diwali,"* as we are just a few days away from it. I wonder if I'll see her at the temple on Diwali?

The thing is, everyone lives their own drama. You, me, everyone... Some are just more melodramatic than others.

Think about your life—think about you. What if you were in a country with no family, only a husband that doesn't take care of you, and a child. No money. No job. What would you do to survive? That's a hard question and a harder answer.

Again, I don't know the truth about this lady or her situation. Nor do I really want to. The one thing I can say is that, I was glad I could be of help, even if it only meant buying her an avocado bagel sandwich in a place where she can take a few moments and steps back from the begging, while sitting at table inside the café, hopefully enjoying her sandwich, out of the rain.

Always, do what you can to help, when you can help. Because you never know when you might be the one needing that helping hand.

WHEN THERE'S NOTHING LEFT
14/Oct/2025 09:08 AM

Have you ever known anybody who's lost everything? Maybe once upon a time they had it all. But then, this happened or that happened—they did this they did that, and they ended up with nothing.

Actually, hopefully, you've never had to witness that take place in anybody's life. And certainly, hopefully nothing like that ever happened to you. But, look around, there is so much homelessness all over the place. People who once had a good job, a decent life, now living on the streets in various formats.

Here in cities like L.A., the homeless crisis has gotten really-really bad. I just saw a news report on CNN where they were interviewing people living on the streets and those who are trying to get them off the streets. In at least one case, in that report, a guy had been on the streets for twenty-two years. And, had no plans of leaving. Sure, a lot of these people are driven to the streets by a mental illness or drug use. But, that does not change the reality of the reality.

I suppose we can blame the condition of the drug addiction at least somewhat on the drug addicts themselves. But again, that does not change what is taking place. And, from this, all the world is left with is a lot of people with lives that are totally destroyed.

Sometimes I see homeless people sitting on bus benches or just wandering around. I often wonder what are they actually doing with their life? I mean, for most of us, we have jobs to go to, we have work to do. We come home and take care of our families. We do what we need to do… Yeah, we may not like everything we have to do. But, we have something to do nonetheless.

But, these people with no home, many of them having absolutely no jobs, nor desiring to get one, what do they do with their days? Doesn't that just mean that their entire life adds up to nothing? I don't know, every time I see one of those individuals, just sitting around doing nothing, it sends me to wondering.

But again, back to the point, have you ever known anybody who has lost everything. Sadly, I've known a couple people that has happened to.

An ideal example is, I think back to this one guy I used to know. He lived in the apartment building that I lived in while I was going to college. He had a job. He had a really nice 1962 T-Bird. And, he was making a pretty good living.

What happened next was kind of one of those things that nobody could have predicted. Him, and a number of the other people that lived in my apartment building, decided to all rent a big ranch house together in Tarzana. It was really a nice house. It had a lot of property. And, not unlike many ideologies that grew out of that era, this group of people decided to come together and live together.

I'm sure I've told this story before, in some place, in some way, in some time… But, as we all were friends, they asked me to move in with them, as well. I guess, thankfully, I could read the tea leaves, and I knew it was not going to be as great of an experience as everybody was anticipating. So me, I just stayed in my apartment.

Sure, I went over and hung out with them all of the time. We were all friends; right? But then, one day, they had all turned in their rent to this one guy who was kind of the rent keeper/banker of the household. What did he do? He took the money and ran. Leaving all of them stranded with no money, and soon being forced out of the house.

Some had families to go to. A side story is, this guy actually bailed on his wife, as well. Left her there all alone. Yeah sure, she was having sex with myself and other people on the side. But???

She, who was a dental hygienist, working for her father who was a dentist, got to move back into the family home. Everybody else, however, was left on their own. A couple of them, got some money from their family and grabbed another apartment. Plus, they already had pretty good jobs.

One or two moved back East to where they had originally come from after their family sent them money to get home.

My one friend, his wife who was also a housemate, left him because he had hooked up with an x-biker check who got kicked out of the MC for some reason, who had found her way into the house. Anyway, as he put it, he was in love with her. I drove him and her up to the mountains above Bakersfield, where his father lived. His father, a crazy old long-haired mountain man who had a thirteen-year-old girlfriend. But, I won't get into that here.

I think it's pretty clear. In other words, don't move into a commune. It never works out well.

But, this one guy—the guy that I am talking about, he planned to stay in L.A. He ended up selling his '62 T-Bird for much less than he'd hoped to get for it. Then, I stopped seeing him. He kind of faded away to nowhere.

A couple of years later, I was driving to Vegas. I stopped off in Barstow, as is the common plan. I gassed up, grabbed something to eat from the drive-through McDonald's, in association with my two large cups of coffee that I used to like to get from that location. And, just about when I was on my way, a guy walks up to me as I was about to pull out of the driveway. There he was, my one-time friend from long ago. I guess he didn't recognize me? But, I certainly recognized him.

As his story goes… …The story he told to me… He said he'd fallen on hard times and wondered if I could give him a couple dollars. Of course, I reached into my wallet and slipped him at twenty. Then, I drove off. Hoping that I had helped his life just a little bit. This, once thriving individual, who had one thing lead to another on him. Now/then, he was broke and homeless, and stuck in Barstow, California.

Whatever became of him, I obviously have no idea. But, this is just one example of what can happen to a life. And, how some people can become homeless.

I think back to my *Zen Filmmaking* brother, Donald G. Jackson. As I've said in many places, he was the greatest squanderer of money I have ever met. He literally burned through millions of dollars in his lifetime. Doing this, while leaving his family, when he died, completely penniless. Had his daughter not purchased a small shack out in Joshua Tree a few years before his death, his wife would have had nowhere to live, as they were soon evicted from the house they had lived in for twenty years after his passing. This, while Don had bought his girlfriends an untold number of Boob Jobs, paid the rent for the apartments for many of them, all while spending money like there was no tomorrow. Again, just an example of what can happen to a person out of nowhere or based upon the lifestyle they choose to live.

I had this dream the other night… I had gone off with some people and we ended up somewhere in one of those dream landscape sort of places where there was a lot of water. It was a very lush, river-filled environment. Yet, it was still urban. For some reason, we got separated, me and my people. I found myself trying to walk back to my hotel, via a lot of obstacles. You know, the whole dreamscape thing.

At one point, I ask this person, (a dream associate), and I was pointed in the direction of my hotel. I was told it was a seven mile walk in a certain direction.

When I finally got there, to my hotel that is, I was informed that I was no longer checked in, and all of my possessions had been discarded. Again, all based in a dream environment.

There I stood, wondering what I was going to do next. I had no money, no cel phone, and my passport was gone. I stood there, in my dream, trying to figure out what to do next. My thoughts were to go to the American embassy and call somebody. But, I couldn't remember anyone's number to call for help. I stood there lost in dream-time, wondering what to do next???

Luckily, I woke up right then. It was all just a dream. Thankfully! But, it did make me think about life and how things can really take you over—take you over very quickly.

I'm sure any of you Negative Nellys' out there will read all kinds of nonsense into that dream. But, at least the truth of the truth is, it was just a dream. And, as many dreams do, it did provide me with some deep insight, and some thoughts about the thoughts of life

For many of you out there, you have a very strong family. And, that's really important! Because, if you're like someone like me, with no blood relatives, if anything negative were to happen to me, I'd seriously be SOL.

Well, I guess I do have some blood relatives. It's just that after my father died back in '68, they all broke ties with my mother and me. So, I've never seen or heard from any of them since that point in time. It's not like I'm a hard guy to find. So, that's all on them… But, before I get too far off track…

I believe it's really important to establish yourself as well as you can. Don't be like my friend Don who just blew through money until he had none left. Then, he died, leaving his wife relatively stranded. Or, like the one once-upon-a-time friend I told you about, who believed he could make something of himself, but ended up homeless.

I think for most of us, our dreams and our hopes are pretty simple. But, on the other side of the issue, I know here in Hollywood, (for example), it has been the longstanding promise of human demise. Demise, for those who chase their dreams here. Meaning, you really gotta be careful about what you dream about, and what you do to actualize that dream.

This all takes us back to the point of life. You really need to be as stable as you can be. …Holding on to that stability, even though it may not provide you with the promise of the promise of that promise you dreamed of receiving. Never let yourself go All In. Because, if you do, you may be All Out.

Just something to keep in mind as you pass through the days of your life.

Remember, it's really easy to lose everything. And, if you have no one to back you up, due to the bad deeds you've done, due to the drugs you take, due to the promises you chase, due to the people you believe in, due to the money you've spent, you may end up all alone and on the street, sitting on a bus bench, thinking about nothing but nothing, and wasting the rest of your life.

ROCK IN THE RICE
13/Oct/2025 08:28 AM

"Rock in the Rice," When I say that it kind of makes me want to make the devil horns with my hand. You know, the heavy metal style hand gesture.

But, that's not really what this piece is about.

To tell the story... I was eating in this restaurant maybe six or eight months ago. I was chewing along, enjoying the meal, when, all of a sudden, I bit into something. BAM! I had bitten into a rock. Ouch!!!

You probably know about this, but every now and then, when you're eating, particularly white rice, they'll be rocks in it. Yes, that's due to the fact that the rice wasn't processed fully and/or correctly... ...Or, the people who were preparing it, just didn't care enough to care. But, whatever the causation factor, every now and then, there'll be a rock in the rice.

I remember the first time that I experienced this. I was eating at this really good vegetarian chili place over on Montana Ave. in Santa Monica, back in the later '70s. The place was really good. I really enjoyed their food there. They didn't serve the alcohol, but if you wanted to, you could go to the liquor store next door and grab a brew. With this, you could enjoy your chili with a beer. I would always go to the liquor store, prior to eating the chili, and grab me my favorite beer at the time, St. Pauli Girl.

Anyway/and in any case, I was enjoying my chilly there one day and BAM I bit into a rock. I spoke to the owner about it, and she apologetically told me, *"That just happened sometimes..."* Back then, I guess because I was still young, and my teeth were really strong, it didn't really do any long-lasting damage. It did hurt. But, it didn't break my teeth or anything.

Here I am, four or five decades later, however, and biting into a rock did my teeth no good. It actually totally broke one of my teeth. I remember spinning it out in my hand. The rock and the part of my tooth. Not good!

A lot of people have asked me, why didn't I sue the restaurant? Or, why don't I sue the restaurant? I guess that's just not who I am. I mean, I tell you, if I were to sue everybody who had wronged me in my life, I don't know if I'd be a rich man, but I know my lawyer would be. As, they're the ones who make all the money from those situations. But, to answer any of your current inquiries, no I didn't sue the restaurant, nor do I plan to.

Anyway, I get to my dentist ASAP. She sends me over to a specialist. They do a root canal on the tooth, and all of that sort of junk. …Trying to save the tooth.

I guess I should interject here, the thing is, for whatever reason, and I have no explanation for it, I have really good teeth. I remember my mother had all kinds of problems with her teeth. My father died too young for me to really know about what was going on with him. But, as far as I go, I haven't even had a cavity in over twenty years. Amazing! So, for me to have a tooth problem, is not only very upsetting, it is an entirely new experience for me.

In any case, they did the root canal, but the tooth continued to bother me. For the past or six or eight months, every time I ate anything, the tooth basically hurt.

Me, I go back into the specialist, they re-X-ray it; do a whole three-sixty-things with some weird sort of machine doing this massive X-ray of my mouth, and they come back with the conclusion that the root of the tooth has a crack. It has to be removed. Damn it!

So, I make an appointment with another specialist. I go to have the tooth extracted, have a bone graft put in, so when it heals in like six months, I can have an implant put in.

This only happened a couple of days ago, so I can't really eat very comfortably yet. And, stuff like that. No chips or popcorn or anything. No fun! At least not yet. I imagine many of you out there may have had a similar experience.

The moral of the story… Think about it… How many times in life are we, (you and I), fucked over by someone or something that we never wanted to encounter. …Something that we never wanted to happen to our life. Yet, it did.

Many times, these circumstances, are brought about by the unconscious, uncaring, or even intentionally hurtful actions of someone else. …People who do not care enough to care that they did not clean the rocks out of the rice. Then what? Answer: It is only us that is left to deal with the consequences. Us, that must pick up the pieces.

I say, as I always say, never hurt anybody. I say, as I always say, live your life as consciously as possible so you will never hurt anyone.

But, after that, all you can do is to endure the pain. Get that tooth pulled. Move on with your life as best as you can. Because, at the end of the day, you will forever be the only one who is truly experiencing your pain.

GONE BUT NOT FORGOTTEN
13/Oct/2025 08:27 AM

    Have you ever had a pair of pants, a shirt, maybe a pair of shoes, that you really-really like. Sure, you have other things to wear, but for whatever reason, you always seem to go and put that something on first; before ever thinking about wearing anything else. I'm pretty sure we've all felt like that about some something, sometime, somewhere along the way.

    Me, just yesterday, I had to toss one of my favorite pairs of shoes. I don't know what it was about them, I can't really give you a clear definition and/or an explanation about the, WHY behind all of that. But, the fact of the fact was, I really liked those shoes.

    Yeah sure, I have some shoes that were way more expensive, and other shoes that were even way more comfortable. But, for whatever reason, I really like those shoes.

    The other day, I was sitting in my optometrist office, getting my yearly checkup of the eyes, and I looked down, and I noticed that the tip of the soul on one of them was starting to peel loose. Sad, I thought, as I sat there in the chair. …These shoes are on their way out.

    Me, as you probably know, I basically only wear what can best be described as, most commonly referred to, as tennis shoes. These were a pair of New Balance 801. I can't even quite remember where I purchased them. But, they've been around for a little while. And they've lasted really-really well.

    The sad fact was/is, as I sat there in that examination chair, I knew this was going to be their last rodeo. Then, the next day when I was collecting all the things for the throwaway and recycle pile, I said goodbye to them. And, they were gone.

Certainly, this isn't my only pair of shoes. I think I have like over a hundred pairs of shoes. I don't know, I guess I'm kind of foolish in that way. I've kind of ended up with a whole lot of clothes and a whole lot of shoes over the years.

I remember a little while back there was this reality TV show, and this one guy was really in love with the shoes he owned. I guess they were all high-end designer shoes, and stuff like that. Anyway, in his apartment in Beverly Hills, he had these long shelves above his couch. And, on those shelves, he had all his shoes lined up. I thought that was pretty funny. ...Somebody who's so in love with their shoes, that they want them to be the first thing that people see when they walk into their apartment.

Me, I actually thought to do something similar to that, just not in my living room. But, I never did. My shoes are just stacked upon each other way too high and way too deep in my closet.

Nonetheless, and all this being said, like I said, sometimes there's just some shoes, and/or that something else, that you really-really like. Then, they're gone.

I won't quote that Cat Stevens song here. You know, where he talks about, *"Your dad's best jeans, denim blue faded up to the sky,"* as I've quoted that passage more than a few times. Great song. Most of all his early work was really-really good. But, it really goes to the point and the premise of all this stuff. It's here, then it's gone, and then we're left without.

That's kind of all the truth of life. And, I'm certainly not saying anything new here. Everybody has said it everywhere before. Nothing lasts forever. But, don't you really find it sad when you've really loved something and then it's gone? I know there's been a lot of those things in my life. I guess this is especially the case, as you get longer in the tooth; i.e.: you get old. With each year, more experiences come and then they go.

Anyway, I of course looked and tried to find another pair of those shoes. But, it looks like New Balance stopped making them. That's happened to me before. I remember there was this pair of shoes... ...You can see me wearing them in the Zen Film, *Vampire Abstracta,* I believe. It was another pair of New Balance. I forget exactly, but I think their number was 480. I do know they were black with the yellow N. Really love those shoes too. Really was sad when they were gone.

But back to these I am talkin' about... No longer available. Not much I can do about it.

Welcome to life. All you can do is love it as long as you can love it.

Anyway, I'll throw it out there to the all of you, if you can find me a new pair of New Balance 801, size 12. Hook me up.

WHEN YOU TRY TO DO THE RIGHT THING
13/Oct/2025 08:26 AM

Have you ever had that experience where you're trying to do something nice for somebody, and it just turns out just the opposite? I imagine you have. I think we've all had some sort of experience, something like that.

Kind of an interesting/funny thing went on with my cats and I just recently…

I don't know if you've ever seen these, but they have these newish stone bath mat sort of things. They're made out of stone, and they absorbed the water from your shower or your bathtub very well. Unlike a rug, that kind of just absorbs the water, and sits there in its wet saturation, these stone bath mats actually soak it all up. And, BAM, it's all gone. …They work really well.

Anyway, and in any case, I thought it would be a great idea to get a smaller version of one of those and put it under my cat's water bowls. That way it would keep things cleaner, and if they spilled some water, which they kind of tend to do sometimes, as my one cat likes to put her paws in the water, and play around with it before she drinks, the water wouldn't just build up on the floor.

So, I ordered it from Amazon. It arrived. And, I put it into place. All good.

The thing was, and I luckily noticed this about a day and a half deep into it being there, is that the water wasn't going down as much as it usually does. My two cats tend to drink a lot of water. And, that's a good thing as you want your cats to be very hydrated.

Anyway, I made a mental note in my mind. I mentioned it to my lady, and she said she didn't really think anything was going on. But me, the one who maintains the cat's water and food and all that sort of stuff, noticed something was not quite right.

Last night, in the evening, I filled up the water bowls and took a very clear note at to where they were in terms of their water level. I said to her, and I said to myself, that if they don't go down very much by the morning, I'm going to have to move the stone bathmat.

Then, last night, I hear my one cat being very vocal all night. He was walking around meowing, saying what to whom, I had no idea? But, he was definitely saying something.

This morning, I get up, and I noticed the water hasn't really gone down at all. So, I pulled the stone bathmat. My one cat immediately jumps down off the bathroom counter and runs to the water and starts drinking. Same water bowl, same location, but for some reason he just refused to drink water when the water bowl was sitting on the stone bathmat. As soon as he was done, my other cat runs up and starts drinking water as well.

Wow! I'm glad I noticed that. I'm glad I took notice of that. Because if I didn't, who knows what would have happened.

Me, I had tried to do the right thing. I had tried to make something better for my cats. But, in trying, in doing so, I had achieved just the opposite.

It's all good now, they've drank a lot of water. But, there was a couple days where they weren't getting fully hydrated. Not—not good.

I don't know??? ...Sometimes you try to make things better for somebody. But, it has just the complete opposite effect. Like I already mentioned, this has probably happened to all of us at one point or another. Maybe you can think of a time where you tried to help somebody or something out, and it just went the opposite.

I guess the big question that comes to mind is—is our trying actually doing something for them, or is it doing something for us? That's a hard one to answer. But, I think it's something you really need to think through before you ever try to do anything for anybody. …Something that they haven't asked you to do.

Just a few rambling thoughts for you to keep in mind.

THE PATH OF YOUR BECOMING
09/Oct/2025 06:45 AM

How far did you get in the Path of Your Becoming? How far have you risen in the path of you becoming all that you hoped to become?

For many/most of us, there is that pinnacle that we wished to achieve. I have known a few who have risen to that place. For most, however, they are nowhere near that life-placement. They have dreams, they have fantasizes, but they never reached that peak. Why? For most, it is because they do not try. No, not really.

I was speaking with this Shop Girl I have known for a year or two. Way back in the way when, when I first got to speaking with her, I asked what else she does but this? …This, work at the shop. She told me she was studying to become a respiratory therapist. *"Wow, that's great,"* I said. *"You will help a lot of people!"* *"Yeah, I can't work here forever,"* she interjected.

So many people I have met throughout my life, they each were going to do something. …Something that they never did. Why? A million reasons, I suppose. But, all they ended being is what they were not. All they were, was what they were. They never climbed up and/or out.

Today, I saw this aforementioned young lady. I asked, *"How's school?"* *"I graduated. I just passed the Boards."* *"Wow, that is so great,"* I exclaimed. *"That is really-really good!"*

"I'll be leaving here at the end of the month," she said. *"Did you get a job,"* I asked. *"Yes at…"* It's a very well-known hospital here in L.A.

There she is, this one-time, semi long-time, Shop Girl. Now, a medical professional. She possesses the ability to help so many-many people. She is on her way to living a great life.

Don't get me wrong, there is nothing wrong with being an employee at wherever... Everyone serves a purpose. But, to truly study and to follow a path that can help so many, that is truly a good thing and a higher calling.

I've watched in life how so many people I have known have wanted to Become. But, they did not. I've witnessed how, especially with this internet generation, some have found a method to make enough money to survive at a relatively high level. At least for a moment. But, youth and beauty and popularity, it is all so temporary. It is all so fleeting. Yet, people get lost in it. That has been the same throughout time. Some people find a way to rise to a level they wish to live at, at least for a moment in their time. And, they dive in, headfirst, never even contemplating that it will not last forever. Then, when it is gone, what do they have?

I do not believe that most people have the desire to live a life based on helpful-service. Most, just want it all handed to them. Most just want what they want. They want to Get to Take. I get it. But, for anyone who studies life, that is just not the way existence is for most of us. At most, that thriving is lived and experienced only for a moment. Then, it is gone, and with that and from that, it is back to the grind.

What am I saying here? What I am saying is that any way you can make an honest living is AOK. There's nothing wrong in that. But, if you can take the time, if you possess the ability to focus, if you can choose a path that not only provides for you and your family, but for the betterment of the all of humanity; isn't that the better way to go?

Good for her! She did it! She has the potential to truly live a good life while helping an untold number of others. What more can you ask for than that?

She is an example to all of us.

* * *
08/Oct/2025 06:59 AM

The moment something is created that is when it begins to get old and deteriorate.

THINGS CAN ONLY GO SO FAR
06/Oct/2025 09:31 AM

Right Now, here in this space in time, in the history we are living in this moment of our Now, there is a lot of change taking place. Some/Many may not like the direction the world is going. But, that is always the case. Whenever there is a movement of change, it will always be loved by some and hated by others. That's just the way it goes.

The thing is, change can only go so far. And, this is where people get lost in their message. They want things to be one way or the other. Okay... That's everyone. But, some/many are so far in favor of the change or against the change that is going on around them that they go all crazy, doing all kinds of stuff to either instigate that change or change the change that is changing—trying to stop it.

In that and because of this, a lot of emotions are enacted and released, and a lot of negative things are done.

If we look back to what was taking place in say the 1960s and well into the 1970s, there was this vast moment of freedom. People, who choose to, were allowed to move away from the norm and express their own definition of Suchness. Thus, people were allowed to experiment and, for lack of a better term, *"Be free."*

Of course, looking to the annal of history, many-many people were opposed to this. Those defined and lost in the, *"Normality,"* of what came before were completely against this new counter-culture that propagated freedom of Mind and Self.

This moment went on for a time. Then what happened? It was gone. That's just the way it is.

If we look back to other points in history, like with the fascism that arose in the 1930s and the 1940s, leading to the holocaust, and the Japanese Imperialism that was taking place around this same period, we see that there was a vast movement towards conservatism and secularization. Though this period of world history also came to an end, it never really left us, it spread out and into the 1970s, on a more focalized landscape, where people, lead by Pol Pot in Cambodia, seeking a homogeneous population, where all those that were considered to be the affluent or the learned were seen as wrong, and, from this, much of the indigenous population of the country was killed off. This too came and went. Though other similar situations, large and small, have continued taking place around the globe.

Now, the world trend seems to be shifting towards a staunch conservatism, where ethnocentric ideals are heartily embraced. That's the movement of now. Some of us who lived through a different, early time, prefer the mindset of that time gone past. But, there's nothing we can do to change the trend that is taking place and bring back that former era. That's just the way it is. That's the way the evolution of humanity has taken place. There are large trends of human consciousness, and you are either for them or you are against them or you just don't care either way.

The things is, though you cannot change these trends, as much as you may want to. And, you may, in fact, hate the trend that is taking place, the one thing you can do is to stay true to yourself. Be the ideal individual that you can be. Sure, you can love or hate what is going on around you; that's human nature. But, you do not have to let it dominate and control your mind, causing you to lose your peace, leading to you doing things that are damaging to others. Because then, all you have become is part of the problem, not part of the solution.

In other words, find the peace within yourself. Maintain that peace. And, never let what is going on outside of you become the dominating factor in your life, causing you to feel and do negative things.

Ultimately, the trends of life are forever changing. There is nothing anyone can do to change that. Loving or hating them is your choice. But, the biggest choice you can make is to not be defined by what is going on outside of yourself. Be more than that. Do not be controlled by something you cannot control.

* * *
06/Oct/2025 08:30 AM

When you are at the top of your game, you don't need to criticize anyone.

If you are at the top of your game, and you do criticize someone, that means that you are operating from a mindset of insecurity and undeserving of your position.

WHAT THEY'LL NEVER KNOW
05/Oct/2025 09:05 AM

I was driving down the street the other day, and like sometimes happens, a thought came to my mind of a time gone past. I'm sure similar things happen to you every now and then. It was a memory of a time when my friend and I had this adventure. *"Adventure,"* is a big word, and this life-event was not all that big at all. It was just a thing that happened in the ever-evolving landscape of our lives. But, *"Adventure,"* sounds good. So...

Anyway, it was just a thing. But, a thing that only he and I experienced. No one else was with us. And, I never told anyone about it, and I doubt that he did, as well. Because, it was no big deal.

Yet, it was a strong enough event to pop back up into my mind all of these years later.

That friend of mine passed-away a few years ago. And, the thing I realized from all of this was that, I am the last one who experienced that experience—who knows about that experience. When I am gone, it will be gone.

Certainly, in my life, that was not the only experience that I only experienced with one other person. And, moving beyond the, *"Me,"* is this thought process, think about how many people, all across the globe, throughout the hands of time, that have had an experience with only one other person. It was known, it was lived, then they died, so what became of the experience?

I'm sure you've had an untold number of experiences, experienced with only one other person, as well. What will become of those experiences when they and you are gone?

For each of us, through all of the experiences, one-on-one or otherwise, that we've had, they hold a place of not only memory in us, but also a place where emotions are generated. I mean, some of these one-on-one experiences

I'm sure we've really liked. Some we've really hated. Some, like the one that stirred my thinking about this, was really no big deal. Yet, it was lived. It was lived by my friend, who is no longer here, and I, who is.

All of these experiences... They mean something to us; to you and to me. But, to no one else. Even if you tell someone about them, that other person was not there. They didn't live it. Thus, they can never truly understand and experience what it meant to you.

So, what do experiences really mean? If they are not charted to the realms of some form of forever; they are here, they are gone, then they are forgotten; lost to time and meaning nothing to anyone.

What do your experiences truly mean?

* * *

04/Oct/2025 03:51 PM

Just because you water some dirt doesn't mean that a plant will grow.

*　　*　　*
03/Oct/2025 09:57 AM

How many things that happened to you in your life would you like to erase from your memory?

How many things that you said or did to others would you like to erase from their memory?

LONG TERM ANGER
01/Oct/2025 12:52 PM

I always find it curious when I encounter a person who is holding onto Long Term Anger. What is Long Term Anger? It is a person being mad at a someone for whatever unreasonable period of time that it may be—be that a week, a month, a year, or years.

Have you ever encountered someone like that? Someone who was mad a someone for an unreasonable about of time? Have you ever been mad at someone for an extended period of time?

We all feel anger. That's a human condition. Some are better at letting go of anger than are others. For most, we get angry for a moment, then we slowly let it go.

As we all understand, there are those momentary incidents of anger, like when someone cuts us off when we are driving, and stuff like that. Then, there are those times, when someone does something to us that really upsets us. For those situations we tend to hold onto that anger for a longer period of time. But, all that holding on does, is to hold us back.

I know in my own life, there have been a few people that I held anger at for an extended period of time. I've been cheated in business deals. I have had things stolen from my life. I've had people tell lies about me. I've been ripped off in the film business. ...Just to name a few... For the people who did those things to me, it's true, I was pissed for a time. But, I always knew that I could not let that situation or that person define me, and my next set of actions. Thus, every time any anger would arise in me, over what that person had chosen to do, I would catch myself and redirect my emotions.

I don't think that too many people have held long-term ill will towards me. I mean, I have spent my entire life consciously trying to help people. Whether that was via Karma Yoga, teaching Yoga and/or the Martial Ats when I was young, all for free, onto trying to help people break into the Film Game later in my life, etc...

I've found, whenever someone got angry with me, it always seemed to be based in a misunderstanding more than anything I consciously did. As I am just not, and never have been, one of those people who sets out to take, steal from, disparage, or hurt anyone or anything in any way, shape, or form.

As the digital age came upon, I found myself at the center of the bullseyes a couple of times. People, who do not know me, never met me, or ever even communicated with me, displaying anger towards me due to something someone else said or proclaimed about me that was not true. I get it, I know that's just the new method, used by some people, to get more clicks, likes, followers, and all that kind of stuff—attacking someone. Yeah, we can all say that is wrong, and they will eventually suffer the karma for what they've done. But, nonetheless, that seems to be, (at least to some), the name of the game anymore.

I always find that the people who buy into that level of BS, and use it as a means to motivate anger within themselves, an interesting breed. I mean, sure anger sends all kinds of adrenaline throughout your mind and body. But, it's not a good feeling. Why does anyone want to feel like that? Moreover, why do they wish to seek out life elements that has nothing to do with them, just to motivate that emotion?

And remember, there are some people who actually set about enacting anger in other people. They do this, I guess, because they get some level of self-empowerment from it. Not good. But, that is the way it is

Also, some people seek out a reason to be angry. They look for a reason to get mad at someone. Then, in some cases, they hold onto that anger for a very-very long period of time. Again, not good. But, that is the way it is.

I know the people I have encountered who follow the path of Long Tern Anger are always the ones who never find fulfillment in their life. The reason for that is obvious. They pursue and embody negativity, and from that they hold themselves back from Becoming. But, tell them that, and it will go to deaf ears.

Overall, the main thing in all of this to keep in mind, is that we need to be able to accept that everyone has flaws. Yes, some are much worse than others. But, in knowing this, we understand that we should never allow a flawed person to be able to take control over our feelings, our emotions, leading to our actions, and causing us to embellish their negative deed in any way. We must be more than that!

So, what can we learn from all of this? Do not allow any anger you feel, no matter what the cause, to take control over your life. Do not let it send you down a road of retribution or vengeance, as then, only your own karma and your own next stage of life will be ultimately affected. Mostly, be more than the person who causes anger to rise up in you.

THE WRONG SIDE OF THE TRACKS
30/Sep/2025 12:05 PM

I was driving down the street today, and I noticed this business that had gone out of business a few months back. It was this café that had the best butter cake. I mean, it was really a joy to eat. Go in there in the afternoon, grab a latte and a butter cake, and it was heaven.

More than just a café, it was a really nicely designed business. They had this great rear patio space where it was just so nice to sit.

Located right on a boulevard, that patio really took you away from the sounds and the drive of the city.

Looking at the exterior of the business today, it was really sad. I guess people have done what some people do, and they pretty much destroy the whole vibe that was left on the exterior of the space. Graffiti, and the art works torn down.

Sad! I don't know why people have to behave in that manner?

I don't know about where you live, but here in L.A., you go down one street and it is very nice, travel a few blocks over, and the neighborhood is just the opposite.

I know I've experienced a lot of that throughout my life.

I live in the hills above the South Bay region of L.A. I've been in the South Bay for over forty years and where I'm living now for over twenty. I grew up in Southcentral L.A., Koreatown, and Hollywood. I also lived in the Valley when I was at the university, so I've been around a little bit. And, it's all the same. One block one way and the next block another.

The thing is… Why is it that way? I mean, is it the people on one block compared to the next? Do some care more and others care less? …Some take care of their space and others do not?

Throughout my life, I've had a large amount of neighbors. Some have been super nice and very considerate and conscience. Others, have been just the opposite and have really fucked with my life. I mean, what is the karma for that? Those who are nice and do good verses those who do not? And, what is the recourse?

I believe that most people who live on the low-level of life, who live from a place of unconsciousness and do things that negatively alters the Life Place of other people are really operating from a space and mindset of frustration, self-loathing, and hating their own life. Because, if you are in a good space in your life, you present that to the world. Yes? You only do good things.

Now, no one can really say what has created any person and/or why they enact their negative behavior. And, if you call them out on it, most will simply deny who and what they are and why they are doing what they are doing. But, if a person does present in that sort of a way, immediately you know who they truly are. That does not change what they may or may not do. But, at least you understand who they are and why they should be avoided.

Life is the complicated interaction of experiences. Many of which are brought on by others.

So, do you destroy the exterior of a once thriving business just because you can? Do you hurt, damage, or destroy anyone or anything? If so, why do you do it? And, what will doing that do to the ultimate reality of your own life? Mostly, do you ever even think about any of this?

The aforementioned business is gone. That is sad enough. Even when it was opened, I always thought if it had been placed in a better environment, a better location, it would have thrived. But, as it was placed on the wrong side of the tracks, what it could grow to was highly limited.

It's gone and its ethos has been destroyed by those who do such things. Sad! I guess that's simply an ideal depiction, and an important lesson in life. Everything… You and I and the all of the everything else is defined by where they/you are located. ...Right side, or wrong side of the tracks.

THE PRICE OF FAME
29/Sep/2025 07:06 AM

Every now and then, I either notice or get a message about something Scott Shaw selling on eBay. Sure, various copies of the books I have written are up there all the time. That's just expected. They don't really catch my attention unless they are some very rare piece of work or a special edition from the publisher or something published in some language that I never knew about and/or never got paid for.

The things that do catch my attention, or my fancy, if you will—the things that I jokingly take notice of are, when someone is selling some rare piece of Scott Shaw something and asking way too much money for it.

I've spoken about this in the past when someone is selling some out-of-print something, like a rare VHS tape. These always make me smile as the sellers are always asking so much money for them. I always say, *"No one will pay that!"* Whether they do or not, I never really know. It's not like I pay all that much attention to the auction or the listing. I know recently there were a few VHS tapes up for sale: A screener copy of *Toad Warrior* and an unopened copy of *Armageddon Blvd.*

The thing that makes me smile about all of this, and the reason I mention this here and now, is (again) the price(s) they ask are so high. I laugh, because I have a bunch of copies of them. Plus, I have the Masters, so I could produce more. If I could get the price that are asking for them, I would be RICH!

Most recently, I was turned on to the fact that someone is selling the original 8.5 X 11 theater card, promo-flyer for *The Roller Blade Seven*. Where they got that, who knows? They were only used at the American Film Market, MiFed, and Cann in 1992 as a means to sell the movie to international buyers. It sold. But, I received nothing. But, that's all another story—one I've talked about in the past, probably way too much. Welcome to Hollywood!

Anyway, they're asking $49.95. Again, this makes me smile. I have a box full for those theater cards. Plus, I threw tons of them away years ago.

I think it's funny—especially from the perspective of someone on the being viewed and auctioned side of, *"Fame."* Fame, for lack of a better term… People speaking about me and selling my STUFF that I've created, or had a part in creating. Strange…

My sister-in-law posted a selfie that she and her kids got to take with Dave Grohl the other night. She's a longtime fan of LCD Soundsystem and went to their show at the Hollywood Bowl last week. …Her teenage kids in tow. There, she apparently ran into Grohl. She was also a major fan of Nirvana back in the day. Seeing them, (Nirvana), as she apparently told Grohl, at the Forum way back in the way back when.

It looks like Grohl actually took the selfie. It's a really good one. Him, her, and her two kids. Me, I take the worst selfies. But, with Grohl as the photographer, doesn't that make it a valuable piece of art in itself?

I hear he's a nice guy. I guess he lives in the Valley, or there adjacent, as every now and then I see photos that people I know take with him. Selfies, the autographs of the New Age.

But, this is L.A., you see celebrities all the time. No biggy. Most celebrities are not so nice, however.

Anyway, back to the point before I get way too far off of the point.

Fame, selling, rarities, and all of that kind of stuff…

You know, if people sell old poster art, and ask a lot of money for it, wouldn't it just seem logical that a singular selfie would be worth so much more? Why don't people sell those on eBay?

It's like this guy contacted me last week about selling some of my art as NFT. Now, to tell you the truth, I don't really understand that whole NFT thing. In fact, I don't understand the whole Bit Coin thing either. But, when I asked him which pieces he was interested in, he pointed to some of the film posters I designed. I DON'T GET IT??? Those pieces are already out there. Anyone can download them. How could they be worth anything? Maybe you can explain it to me???

Anyway… The point to all of this… Fame is a weird commodity. It seems it makes money. But, money for that someone else who is not famous rather than the person who is. And, like in the case of Dave Grohl, he can't even go to a concert without people coming up to him and asking for a selfie.

What is the price of fame? What is the cost of fame? And, why does everyone seemingly seek it out?

SPEAKIN' ABOUT
WHAT I WAS SPEAKIN' ABOUT
27/Sep/2025 06:18 AM

  I was kickin' back here on a Friday night. Another bottle of the grape gone down. Post a Rom Com, (that I like to call a Ro Co). ...Films that my lady likes to watch. After the fact, I click over to the music video stations. Immediately, I hit onto MTVs Metal Mayhem, and on the TV, playin' their music, is a band that used to rehearse and have their guitar work done at the shop I was just discussin' in the last blog gone past.

  The guy playin' lead guitar, was paying a guitar made by my friend, who made mine, (in the blog post last). There it was, in full view, for the world to see.

  That player passed away from AIDS, as did more than a few of the people I knew—way back in the way back when. SAD! If you weren't there, you could never understand. So many people died.

  For the more contemporary of you out there, it was in someways like COVID-19, loved-ones here then gone. Sad, sad, sad! So many lost.

  The guy rocked his lead though very well, in the aforementioned song playin' on the TV. It's a good song. Though I can't say I was ever a fan of that band. Or, of many of the Hair Metal bands of that era. But, I can say that it was a TIME. A time that if you weren't there and livin' it, you could never truly understand.

  My lady, who knows, via me, the creator of that guitar, (and mine, the one discussed from the that last blog post made), asked me what happened to him? Him, the creator of that guitar. Why did he fall from grace? A question I have also asked. As once upon a time he was the man—the king of a kingdom. A place where many of the guitar-gods of the era came to have their guitars fixed, modified, and created. ...A question I asked of the man himself. I mean, he was the man of an era. The place to go to get your guitar did. Like he told me, and now I tell you, times change. Factories took over the reins. The guitarist, who were actually a someone, went straight to the source. The name-brands made them their guitars to the standards and specifications they wanted. Thus, his masterful one-off creations fell out of fashion.

That does not change the contribution he made to an era, however. A contribution you had to be there to appreciate. He, and his staff, worked and reworked a lot of guitars for a lot of people. How many guitars did he make and/or modify for me? A lot! Wish I still had them all.

But there, locked in history, is at least one of them. Making music on the TV screen that is still listened to today.

Me, all this made me smile. Me, a lover of guitars to this day. I just purchased another one this AM.

But, that's not really the music I focus on creating anymore. I would rather fall into the perfection of Zen and work within in the electronics of music. Where every note is a new expression of Suchness. A note that may never be played again. ...Kind of like freeform jazz, I think. Only true to the moment. Perfection within imperfection.

Not like guitar. Not like Rock. Where every note must be rehearsed and then played over and over and over and over again, each time a song is actualized.

It was great then. But, it is so far from Zen now. ...At least for me.

The video was over. The guy who played the notes on the guitar, made by my friend, long gone. Then, it was all gone. The player, the song, the notes, the video.

I flipped the station. Flipped over to a more pop influenced presentation. A great song was playing. No guitar was featured. Just a guy and girl, doing what a guy and a girl do. The age of Rock is over.

All this is a lesson in life. Remember, times change. Nothin' stays the same. What may be our bread and butter today, may not feed us anything tomorrow. We, (you and), can hold onto what once was. We can hold on as long as we can hold on, if that is what you or I hope to do. But, no matter how much we hold on, that does not stop the change. Like the lyric from the theme song from the great 1960s film, *Wild in the Streets, 'Nothin' Can Change the Shape of Things to Come.'* Remember that.

*   *   *

27/Sep/2025 06:15 AM

You can shift the blame to someone else when a situation does not turn out the way you had envisioned.

But, by shifting the blame, don't you remove the fact that you chose, at least initially, to be a participant in what actually unfolded?

FUNNY STORY—FLASH BACK
25/Sep/2025 02:30 PM

I'll tell you a funny story. At least I think it's a funny story…

I was going through all of my guitar parts today. Doing a Spring Cleaning in the Autumn.

The thing is about guitar parts—that is if you work on guitars, creating, redoing, remaking, modifying, and all of that kind of good stuff, you never know what you will need until you need it. If you have it, great! If not, then you have to go and find it, (and get it), which takes time and breaks your flow and all of that kind of nonsense. No Fun. So you, meaning me, and others of my nature, we collect a lot of screws, nuts, bridges, pickups, pickguards, tunning keys, knobs, you name it…

Anyway, my STUFF had gotten a bit unruly, so I decided to go through it all and clean it up. In doing so, what I found was my favorite guitar pick from the 1970s. WOW, I did not even know that it still existed. Yes, I, of course, remember it. But, I thought it was long gone. It was not. It still had the logo from West L.A. Music on it. A place where, back in the day, was one of the few and the best places to get your (my) gear.

In any case, I've always played very light guitar picks. In fact, I play the lightest gage picks I can find. That's always been my style. Whereas, many/most players go for a thicker gage. Back then, very thin picks were a bit hard to come by. So, that pick was/is a unique piece of history. At least in my mind.

Finding it, sent me down memory lane. And, here comes the funny story. Finally… That, at least I, think is funny.

Back when I first got into the Film Game, when I was in my early thirties. My agent would send me on a lot of auditions. I got this one for a commercial, where they were seeking a heavy metal guy who could really play great lead guitar. Right up my alley. Though the fact to the fact is, many a person has assumed that I'm into Metal, due to the length of my hair, but that's not the actually the case.

So, I go to the audition, guitar in hand. Ahead of me were all of these long-haired players. Now, I'm not saying they were all bad. But, most of them were actors, and not true musicians. Which was the complete opposite of me. They got up there, read their lines, and played their licks, with little consequence. Nothing great. Finally, my turn. The last guy up for the part. I go up there, and I just burn up the lead. I mean, that's what I do/did. I was a hot-licks lead guitarist. Though my guitar playing influences did not come out of Rock, but came from people like Jon McLaughlin and Al Di Meola, add a little distortion to my sound, and I could blow it up.

I concluded. I could tell the casting agents were blown away. I look at them, and in all my knowing arrogance say, *"I guess I get the gig."*

Thinking back, I remember I brought the guitar to that audition made by my friend Jim Foote. It was a great player. Really definitive of the era. Strat style, single humbucking, Floyd Rose. It had this awesome crack-o-lite finish on it done by a guy named Jim O'Connor. I wish I still had that guitar. I think I got poor at one point, and needed some money, so I sold it. If the guy I sold it to still has it, and wants to sell it back to me, let me know, I give you the four-hundred dollars you paid me for it.

I didn't hear anything for a couple of weeks. I was really surprised as I felt I had really nailed the part. Then, one night, I'm watching TV with my lady, and a commercial comes on. I believe it was for Doritos, if my memory serves me right. There, instead of me was Ted Nugent doing the part. I both laughed and was a bit annoyed. I got beat out by a Rock Star. Even though I think I'm a better player than he is. My question was, why did they even bother auditioning me and others if they knew they were going to cast him. But, as I learned, that's Hollywood.

There's a lot of things that could/can be read into this on all levels. But, anyway… Just a note from the *Annals of Scott Shaw*. A little piece of history and perhaps a little bit of a life lesson, for whatever it is worth. Make of it what you will.

* * *
25/Sep/2025 07:10 AM

You ask a person for their advice.

They give you their advice.

You decide to follow their advice.

Can you blame them when you don't like the outcome of you following their advice?

PSYCHIC OR NOT
24/Sep/2025 01:11 PM

If I can reference one of the very tongue-in-cheek lines we created in *The Roller Blade Seven* as the title for this piece… Psychic or Not?

I was driving home today, and I passed by this relatively newly-developed, *"Psychic,"* compound. The structure was/is a very large, older ranch-style house that had been converted into a business front years ago.

About a year ago, this female, *"Psychic,"* moved in and completely renovated the interior and the exterior of the property. It had to cost a lot of money. Every time we, my lady and I, would drive by, would comment as such.

As the months went on, I always wonder where all of her business was, as she seemingly had none. The parking lot was always empty, and the sign always said, *"Closed."* Then, today, I drive by, and I see a massive, *"For Lease,"* sign on the building. I guess she wasn't that great of a Psychic. She didn't see that after spending all of that money to renovate the place that she would have no business and would have to go out of business.

I remember a number of years deep now. I was driving down the street and there was one of those digital billboards, and on it was the statement. *"Psychic Faire, Cancelled."* My lady and I looked at each other and laughed. *"I guess none of them were psychic enough to know that their event would be cancelled."*

Earlier today, I was writing about the fact that we all have to be careful about those who call themselves a teacher. I believe a, *"Psychic,"* is the ultimate example of that.

…Like I always say, if you want to truly test a so-called psychic, ask them a question about yourself or your family that there is no possible way that they could know the true answer. And, when they dodge the question, get it wrong, or make excuses for their inability to get it right, then their truth will be revealed.

Life is an interesting process. We all want to know answers to questions that we want the answer to but can never truly have. The list of those questions is a vast as the number of humans on this planet at any one point in time. But, turning to someone, and paying them, to answer those questions, always comes with a question of truth.

Some people just want to believe, and that's their mistake.

So, like I illuded to earlier in the previous blog, *"Be careful of who you listen to and why you listen to them."* If you ask someone/anyone a question, sure, maybe they can pretend to have an answer. But, the only true answer to anything is what is inside of your own Inner Self.

Remember, only you can know the true answer to you.

AN UNWORTHY VESSEL
24/Sep/2025 04:48 AM

I had kind of a funny experience the other day...
...At least I find it funny. Someone asked me if I would be their teacher. Not in the sense of the martial arts or filmmaking or hatha yoga or something like that, but in the sense of spirituality. I just said, *"That's not me."*

Now, if I can walk this back a little bit in time. I believe the first time someone asked me to be their, *"Teacher,"* or as their put it, *"Guru,"* was when I was about twenty years old.

To tell the story, I was teaching a course on the various aspects of yoga at the extension college at California State University, Northridge. Where, I was also a student. I've written about this in other places, but I was teaching the course using my sanyass name, Swami Mokshananda, which I preferred back then, and it was a young couple trying to find their way on the Path. I invited them over to my apartment in Tarzana, offered them some tea and the like, as we sat on the floor, (I had no furniture to speak of), and we spoke about life, and spirituality, and... My answer to them, *"No."* Nicely put, of course. But then, as now, I am not so ego driven to call myself a teacher.

I've spoken to people on this subject more than I have written about it. Though I have covered in via the typing keys, as well. Pretty much, anyone who claims to be a teacher is never a true teacher. All they are is an ego-driven individual who wants to rock their superiority over others by falsely believing that they know something that you or I do not.

And, that's pretty much it. Look at all the so-called teachers, gurus, priests, ministers, swamis, you name it—by whatever name you can conjure up, and they've all fallen short and been found out to be fakes. Fakes, at least in terms of the truth of purity and righteousness, and all of that good stuff. That's why people turn to and believe in avatars and the proclaimed beings of times gone past. They are gone. And, all that is left of them is their promised legacy. The tales of how true, and great, and holy they were. But, they are not here. They died eons ago. There is no way for the living to know how truly holy they actually were. Yet, the myth lives on. And remember, that is all it is, a myth.

Many people seek the deeper meaning in life. Myself included. But, you need to be carful about who is saying what and why.

So, think about this whenever you meet someone who is a so-caller teacher—anyone who claims they know something that you do not. Anyone who promises you anything but puts a price tag on it. If they truly were a teacher, they would never claim to one. And, they certainly wouldn't put a price tag on it.

*   *   *
21/Sep/2025 04:06 PM

If someone you didn't know walked into where you live, what would they think?

FOR THOSE WHO DON'T PRACTICE
19/Sep/2025 03:59 PM

I don't know if you ever played sports, or did the martial arts, danced ballet, played a musical instrument, or anything like that, but the one thing that the coach or the instructor emphasizes over-and-over again is that you must practice. You must keep retuning to the basics and do your techniques again and again.

Most people don't like to do that. They just want to get out there and DO IT. This is especially the case in say a physical activity like the martial arts. Once a student is getting better at the craft, all they want to do is to unleash the advanced techniques. They want to show off their skills. They don't want to look like a beginner and do the basics.

The problem with this mindset is, however, all of the advanced techniques, in any skillset, are based on the basics. The more you perform these basic techniques, the deeper one grows in understanding. And, from this, the better their advanced techniques have the ability to become.

This understanding is not simply for the physical activities of life. It goes out to the all and the everything.

I know as a filmmaker, one of the biggest obstacles I have encountered is a cameraman who does not know how to use the camera with any level of proficiency. Pretty much, since day one in my emergence into the filmmaking game, I have witnessed how often the cameraman truly harms a project by not knowing how to truly use the camera. Why don't they know how to use it? Because they do not practice.

Like I've proclaimed forever, one has to develop the ability to see what the camera sees. Not just what the human eye sees. But, how the camera captures the world, is a very different beast from what is seen by the human eye.

How does one do that? Practice.

I don't know if it is simply based in laziness. Or, if it is based in an individual believing they are somehow better than they actually are. Whatever the case and the motivation, what occurs from one not practicing is that whatever is done, it becomes not nearly as good as it could have become if one had practiced.

So, this is just something for you to think about. Think about as you pass through your life. How much do you practice? How much time do you actually spend becoming the best that you can be by going back to the basic, and then moving up from there, doing and redoing, trying and retrying until you truly master whatever it is that you hope to achieve.

*　　*　　*

18/Sep/2025 03:55 PM

If you take something from someone, you owe them.

It's as simple as that.

If you accept a gift from someone, you owe them.

It's as simple as that.

If you learn something from someone, you owe them.

It's as simple as that.

If you steal something from someone, you owe them.

It's as simple as that.

Most people are all about the receiving. They quest for what they want. But, few people ever truly understand the cost of their getting.

NOBODY OWNS THEIR ACTIONS
18/Sep/2025 03:29 AM

I was just closing my eyes this evening, when crash! I hear glass shattering.

Awoken, my lady and I seek out what has gone on.

As it turns out, it looks like my lady had placed one of the ancillary cat drinking bowls on the side of the kitchen counter. A place where one of our cats jumps up to periodically. And, not knowing it was there, our cat sent it crashing to the ground. Glass everywhere.

We get up and we sweep it up.

No big deal in the overall reality of life. But, it was a bit of an annoyance.

The cat ran and hid under the bed. Our other cat, also wandering/wondering what went on, stood there watching the clean-up.

You know, the smashing of that glass bowl is an ideal example of life. It's here. Then, someone does something, (accident or not), and then it's gone.

The culprit runs and hides. Denying responsibility. But, that does not mean that they did not do it.

There's a lot going on in the right about now here in the U.S. There are assignation attempts. And, there are assignations. But, the big issue is, no matter where you stand on the love or the hate on the like or the dislike of anyone or anything what gives you the right to be the judge and jury leading to the hurting or anyone or even the ending of their livelihood or life? Don't you think that is pure vanity to believe you have the right to judge anyone? Yet, isn't it done all the time?

If we look to the media, at least here in the U.S., it has become so polarized. It is no longer the news. It's just simply someone stating what they feel and presenting it as a fact. But, an opinion is never a fact.

Just today, a prominent satirist's and late-night TV show host had his TV show pulled from the Air Waves due to his comments on the recent assignation of a Right-Wing Influencer.

The thing is, and this is something that really needs to be thought-out by each individual, is that here in the U.S., we are promised the right to Free Speech. But, the problem with that promise is that Free Speech, directed by someone who does not hold the knowledge of a God is no more than an opinion. And, if the person exercising their Free Speech spreads their negatively-based opinions to others, it has the potential to cause other people to murder. Like what happened a couple of days ago.

This is where discretion, known in Sanskrit as, Viveka, and wisdom, known in Sanskrit as, Prajñā comes into play.

People who do not possess a deep sense of understanding, spout their beliefs everywhere. Some have even gained a platform for doing so. But, if what they speak sends out a current that causes negativity to rise in the masses, then what have they done? All they have done is to hurt the reality of one person, leading to damaging the actuality of more people. Thus, creating a world where hurt, damage, and even death is instigated.

Think about your own life, what words have you spoken, what opinions have you vocalized that have hurt the life of someone/anyone? If what you have said, based upon what you have believed, has hurt anyone, what are the consequences? Shouldn't there be some?

Really, ask yourself this question. Study the reaction(s) you have unleashed. From this, what was given birth to? A better world? Or, a world where someone is hurt or even killed?

It seems that in many cases, people do damage and do not care about the damage they have unleashed. They are not fired from their job as has been the case of a number of people who have recently expressed glee about the murder of that Right-Wing Commentator on social media. They are not put on leave by their network, as they have offended a large portion of their audience like the aforementioned TV host. But, as they received no repercussions as to what they have done, that does not mean that they are free and clear.

What they have created is a world where hurt is actualized. And, from this, all of the world/all of humanity is made that much less.

And, when their turn comes to suffer their karma, what do they do? They cry out, telling the all and the everyone just how poor and hurt they are. But, they are the ones who created this world of hurt. They are the ones who instigated and unleashed this pain.

So, this is just some thoughts. A moment to look around you and to consciously view the condition of the world. See the pain. View the murder. Witness the reprisals for the words that hurt.

How have you participated? And, if you have participated, in any negative manner, what are you going to do about it? Just wait for your karma to come calling? Or, are you going to suck it up, fix what you have broken, and actually make this world a better place?

SOMEBODY DIDN'T GET THE MEMO
17/Sep/2025 06:05 AM

Whenever I am in Europe, it truly dumfounds me the amount of people that still are smoking cigarettes. I mean, the information is out there. It is really-really bad for you. It will kill you. And, it not only hurts you but all of those around you, via second-hand smoke. Plus, by throwing all of your used cigarette butts on the ground, it truly pollutes the environment. But yet, there they are. Everyone is smoking.

I spend the last week or so in Berlin. And, there it was again. Everyone smoking. Many a person was walking down the street with a cigarette in their hand. Blowing their smoke into the air. Polluting the air of everyone else. I saw people eating in cafes, a cigarette in one hand and a fork in the other. I mean come on! You have to take a drag between every bite? I even saw this one very pretty young couple sitting on the banks of the Spree, as concrete as they are, making out. The girl half of the couple had a cigarette in her hand. Why?

I remember back in my younger days, when I would meet a girl that I liked and she smoked. Man, that was a horrible flavor in her mouth when we would kiss. I'm sure I mentioned that in some piece of poetry or something, way back in the way back when, Cigarette Kisses. Horrible!

Here in the U.S... And, don't get me wrong, I'm not saying we are better or anything. But, there is many a city where a person cannot smoke on the streets in public anymore. Restaurants and even bars, forget about it. No-go. And, that's a good thing!

I mean, just look at the skin of a person who has smoked throughout their life. Compare them to someone of the same age, as they move deep into their life, and the difference is obvious.

My mother who smoked since she was sixteen had horrible lines in her face when she reached her later years.

Compare her to my aunt and uncle who were both many years older than her, they looked so young for their age. No smoking. No lines.

I don't know??? Maybe you can explain it to me??? I just don't get it??? All of the facts are out there. Cigarettes kill. Yet, so many people are still smoking.

They strongly aided in my father's death from a massive heart attack at the age of only forty-eight. My father-in-law literally died from lung cancer at sixty. And, I know of several other people who died either directly from or passed away way too young at least in part due to their smoking. It's not cool. It doesn't make one look cool. It provides no true benefit to anyone's life. All a person who smokes is doing is slowing killing themselves and hurting the life or others and the environment while throwing away their money and putting it in the pockets of the tobacco companies.

Smoking has been proven to be an addiction that is very hard to break free from. Why do it? Yet, like in Berlin, virtually everyone I saw had a cigarette in their hand or was waiting to have a puff. Why?

Did someone not get the memo?

THE GOD CONCEPT
08/Sep/2025 12:20 PM

    First of all, I am not here trying to make anyone angry or to challenge anyone's system of belief. What I am presenting in this piece is simply just a little food for thought.

    Pretty much, from the moment we are born, we are programmed into believing in a higher power. Though this higher power is defined by many names, via the various cultures across the globe, by whatever name you name it, it is that grand being that we are taught to turn to in times of need and to ask forgiveness from when we know we have done something wrong.

    I know, being born into and raised in a Christian family, from my earliest memories forward, I was taught that I must pray each night, ask for forgiveness for my sins, and to always have the thought of God in mind in all that I do. Certainly, this is not necessary a bad thing. But, what occurs from this style of schooled life-development is that one is programmed into believing. One is taught what they must think and how they must think it.

    Hand-in-hand with this style of religious programming comes all kinds of subtitles of what you must do and what you must not do. How you should behave, what you should say, how you should say it, and what you shouldn't say or do. I have studied this in myself, and no matter how far I can intellectually separate myself from this programed mindset, it is always somewhere in there, deeply hidden in the back of my mind. This is why when many a proclaimed atheist is about to pass away; they regain their belief in God. They need something to believe in/something to hold onto, as they proceed through the most complicated passageway of life.

    All this being said, is what we are taught the truth or is simply what we are taught to believe? Yes, there is a difference. And, just because someone else believes it, and tells us it is the truth, does that actually make it the truth?

Recently, there was a horrific mass casualty event here in the U.S. A crazed gunman took his weapon to a Catholic church and shot into a group of children partaking in Mass. Some were killed; many were injured. It was terrible. An event like that should never have been allowed to happen.

I had the chance to speak with a South Korean-born Christian minster the other day. I asked him, *"If there was a God, why would he let that happen?"* His immediate answer was, *"Because they did not have enough faith."*

This answer made want to scream. But, I simply replied, *"They were children. How can anyone judge them on how much faith they possessed? They were at church. They were going to Mass. They were doing all the right things in step with their religion. Why didn't God protect them?"*

His answer, *"It's all about faith. Believing, means you believe in God's ultimate wisdom."* But, what does that even mean? Believing in a God that allows his children, his disciples, to be brutally murdered. How is that right or holy on any level?

I believe if we look around the world, at any place where any religion is practiced, we can see horrible things take place to all of the Believers from time to time. No one religion is safe. No one Believer is safe. And yes, there are all of the answers propagated by the pundits of any religion, giving reasons why one should still believe no matter what takes place. But, shouldn't the entire promise of the concept of God, keep the Believers protected?

Religion is a very complicated subject. Still to this day, one religion hates and judges another. Even within one single overshadowing creed or school of thought there is dissension and attacks. That does not make it right. That does not make it the way it should be. But, that is the way it is.

Add to this, people of a lower mind. People who actually set out to hurt others. In truth, isn't it the truth, that something like that is wrong on all levels of understanding. An individual who is a Believer in a God doing bad things to others? Yet, as in the case of the attack on the children at that church last week, it goes on all over the place all of the time.

Ask yourself, how much of a participant are you in the goings-on of your life and of the life and lives taking place around you that would be against what you have been taught by your religion?

The thing is, people do what they do, motivated by whatever self-serving ideology they may possess. And yes, maybe they believe in a God or in the religion they were programmed into. But, that does not necessarily stop them from doing bad or negative actions.

In many cases, religion promises forgiveness for the bad actions of its faithful. But, how can asking a priest or a God for forgiveness remedy any negative deeds you, or anyone else, has done? All that is, is selfishness. All that is, is self-thinking-ness. By acknowledge what hurtful action you have unleashed and seeking forgiveness for those deeds, in a confessional or elsewhere, is simply you (or anyone) wanting to feel better about a bad deed that you chose to unleash. But, what have you actually done to undo what you have done to the life of that someone else? To fix what you have broken?

People are programmed into believing in a higher power. They are taught to live by the rules of whatever religion they are indoctrinated into. But, does looking to God in a time of need always work? Does asking God for forgiveness change anything about what you have done? And, if there is a God, why would he allow the children of his (or her) faithful to be slaughtered?

Ask yourself these questions before you believe.

*   *   *
08/Sep/2025 12:20 PM

You can change your mind.

*   *   *
07/Sep/2025 08:09 AM

If a doctor gave you anywhere from six months to one year to live, what would you do with your remaining time?

Most people live their life as if they will have tomorrow. If you understand that this is not the case, then maybe you will focus your life on only doing the things that truly matter to you.

PEOPLE ARE WHO THEY ARE
05/Sep/2025 07:28 AM

When was the last time you got really mad at someone? ...Really mad at someone for something you believed that they did?

When you got mad at them, did you ever question, *"What is my responsibility in what happened?" "What part did I play in this outcome that led to my anger?"*

Here is a fact about life, and a fact that few people choose to realize, people are who they are. All you have to do is to be aware enough to study who they are, what they do, how they interact with you, and how they interact with other people, and you will know what to expect.

For example, did you ever listen to the stories told by this person about their relationships with other people, before you became angry with them? If you did, most likely you would have been able to see what was coming between you and them. You would have been able to gage how their relationships with other people evolved and ended.

...Did you ever look at the life of the person you became angry with, before you became angry with them? What had they done prior to your/that interaction? Where are they in their life? Did they have established friendships, a stable lifestyle, and an established career? Or, was their life lost in the wind?

Again, people are who they are.

Yes, some people do lie about who and what they are. But, even when this is the case, if you take the time to study them, (their behavior, and their lifestyle), you will be able see through the illusion they present long before it becomes a problem.

What is anger? What is anger focused on another individual? Basically, it is based upon the fact that you do not like what that other person did. Now, this can be a small thing, or this can be a very large thing. But, the fact of the fact is, whenever you are angry, it is you who chooses to instigate that emotion in yourself. Thus, anger is always your choice.

This is not to say that it cannot be motivated by what someone does. But, it is you who chooses how to react to that life incident.

So, what does this tell us? The fact of life is, not everyone is going to behave in the way you want them to behave. People are going to do things you do not like. Though they may be the one to instigate the factors that created the emotion of anger within you, it is only you who chooses what you with that emotion.

A lot of bad things have been done based in anger. A lot of people have been hurt, and a lot of negative karma has been set in motion.

Ultimately, if you choose to feel the emotion of anger, (and it is a choice), what you do with it can not only come define the rest of your life but the rest of all those who encounter the reverberations of your anger. Thus, though someone else may have instigated what you are feeling, if you cannot keep that emotion under control and perhaps even transcend it, in may damage the next evolution of your life.

* * *
04/Sep/2025 06:44 AM

If you honestly made a list of all of the bad things you've done; all of the people you've hurt, all of the harmful, hurtful, or selfish actions you have made, would you be allowed into heaven?

BEGGIN' FOR A DOLLAR
03/Sep/2025 02:00 PM

In India, if a holy man comes up to you and requests food, (or anything), it is almost considered a necessity that you give it to him. Not only does it help the person walking the holy path, but it is believed that the Giver will receive good karma for doing so.

This practice is known as, *"Bhiksha,"* in Sanskrit.

Now, this is not to say that there are some who take advantage of the process. I've seen Westerners there, dressed in the clothing of a holy man, following that path. But, I'm sorry, they come from a wealthy nation. They should not be there putting more stress on an already strained populous. This, no matter what path they think they are walking. It is not helping. Go home and get a job!

Of course, this practice of begging is totally looked down upon in the West. Though some people go out of their way to help these people out, many immediately rebuke them.

I had to go to the dentist this AM. As I was driving home, I realized I hadn't had anything to eat. It came to me to go to my local Starbucks and get one of their tasty grill cheese sandwiches and I latte—non-fat, of course.

I ordered it on the app, so it would be ready when I got there. Went inside. Grabbed it. And, decided to go and eat it out on the back of the shop, on their patio that overlooks the Pacific. All good.

As I was sitting there, I noticed his one lady come up to an elderly gentleman. She began to give him a spiel about how she had to wait a week or so for her son to get to her and she was in need of money, and stuff like that. It just made me smile…

The backstory to all of this is that this woman is in the large parking lot of this shopping center, where Starbucks is located, all the time. It was like six months ago, or more, that she came up to me asking for money. Same chatter, different day.

This lady is probably in her late thirties or early forties. I believe she is of South Asian descent, due to her slight accent.

But, the thing of the thing is, I can't image how profitable that parking lot is for her. I mean, if I recognize her, I'm sure a lot of other people do, as well. I've seen her ask a lot of people for money. But, just like that elderly gentleman of today, I've never seen her receive anything. So, what is the point? It's not some holy quest so she can eat so she can meditate. I guess she's getting something out of it, or she wouldn't be coming back. But, her entire process leaves me in question. Why???

And, I guess that is the ultimate question in life, *"Why?"* Why does anybody do what they do? Why do they do it if is somewhat off of the norm? What do you do? And, why do you do it? What does what you do give back to society and the world, and what does it take away?

Do you ever question this question? If not, maybe you should.

THE WIND THROUGH MY HAIR
30/Aug/2025 02:03 PM

Yesterday, I had to move my motorcycle around a little bit. So, I did a little bit of driving it here and there with no helmet on.

At least here in Cali, it is the law that you must wear a helmet which driving your motorcycle. It has been that way since I believe 1991. I know there are some states, like Arizona, where a helmet is not required. I also know that is the state with the highest rate of motorcycles deaths and injuries in the country.

But, just in my little bit of putting around yesterday, I was reminded of just how free it feels when you ride a motorcycle with no helmet. Just in those few moments it was so freeing.

Back in the day, before helmets were required, I never wore one. It was such a feeling, to be jamming along, the wind in my hair—just so free…

But, like many others, I paid the price. I mean, when I was twenty-one years old there was a girl who caused a major accident with me and I was very close to death. My skull fractured in a million places. My bones broken and my body bruised. I was never the same. My entire life, since that point when I was twenty-one, was defined/redefined by that accident.

I am told it was young lady behind the wheel of her parent's Mercedes, who caused the accident. Do you think she ever thinks about it? Doubt it. Do you believe, all these years later, she even remembers? Probably not. But, she came close to killing me and, most certainly, she changed the rest of my life, in a negative way, forever.

Had I been wearing a helmet, would the outcome have been different? Most probably. But then, like yesterday, the feeling of not having one on was/is so free.

…And, of course, that's not the only motorcycle accident I have had. They are dangerous!

I don't really ride my motorcycle very much anymore. It just seems, that of late, everyone just drives so badly—so self-thinking and self-centered. I am frequently getting run out of the lane and stuff. That does not mean that I do not miss the once-upon-a-time. That feeling of freedom. Of climbing on the bike, kickstarting it, taking off, and riding in the wind.

I guess that's the thing about life. There is the life we want to live. Maybe even the life we remember once living. Then, there is the reality of where we find ourselves in our current life. What once was, can never be again. Though we may have moments where we can relive the memory, once it is gone it is gone, and it will be gone forever.

So sad. But, so true.

THE SOUND OF SILENCE
AKA EARBUDS EVERYWHERE
29/Aug/2025 12:56 PM

So often, when I am out in public, I notice people with earbuds in their ears. I mean, I get it. There are all kinds of reasons why you want to block out the world. But, there is another level to this whole thing. By blocking out the world, not only do you leave yourself venerable to a surprise attack, but you miss out on all of the sounds of nature, of life, and all of that kind of stuff.

I guess, you can kind of call me paranoid. You wouldn't be the first. But, from the way I came up, you always had to be ready. You never knew where the next attack may be coming from. And, you certainly wouldn't want to miss your chance at self-defense. Or, to keep it from happing at all, if you could anticipate the on-coming. Earbud bock all of that out.

I know… I know… Everybody doesn't think that way. They've never had to worry about such things. And, that's a good thing. But, the reality of the reality is, negative things can happen to anyone. And, you should be prepared. I mean, is listening to the same song, that you have heard a million times before, all that important?

But, more than that. The sounds of life, nature, and reality, it's all very interesting. I mean you can learn so much about human psychology, about the nature of man and woman, about life, if you just listen. That's not to mention all of the beautiful sounds of nature and stuff. I mean, there are so many sounds out there. So much to listen to. Human or manmade it is all very unique and interesting if you just listen.

Anyway, that's just my thought(s) for the day after being in a store today, where I just saw so many of the people hiding from reality via wearing their earbuds.

Do you really want to miss out on life?

HOW THE INTERNET FORGETS YOU
28/Aug/2025 04:42 PM

Kinda funny/interesting... As you may remember, yesterday, I was discussing how the main page for the Zen Film, *Guns of El Chupacabra* has fallen out of Google. I mean, it is totally nonexistent on Google. Like it never existed. Even though there are tons of sites that point to it.

Though that strikes me as strange, I won't rehash it here. What I will mention is that I just came to notice how my webpages devoted to the history of the martial arts are no longer coming up in the search for the subject. Google, still knows they are there. But, I guess, I would have to dive way deep to find them...

Once upon a time, in the long ago and the far-far away, if you searched anything about Hapkido and/or Taekwondo the pages on my site would be one of the first referenced on Google. I mean, back then, like today, I have tons of info on the arts.

Now, for example, search, The History of Hapkido, The History of Taekwondo, The History of the Korean Martial Arts, or lessor known subjects like the Korean sword art of Kumdo and my stuff is nowhere to be found. What is found, is a lot of people presenting segments of my research, (as I was the actual researcher), but giving me no credit. They also grab stuff from other people, with no actual reference to them.

There is no deep personal research in what they present. Just a book report at best. But, that's what comes up. Why?

In some ways, I guess I could look at all of this as a good thing. I mean, back in the day, if someone didn't like something I wrote, as truthful as it may be, they would come at me guns blazing and talk all kinds of shit about me on the various sites where such attacks could be posted. But, I am the source. I am the researcher. I was the one who traveled to the source and did the investigation. The research that no one else was doing at the time.

I mean, sure, all of the articles I wrote for magazines will be out there, (somewhere), forever. And, my books on Hapkido and Taekwondo are still in print. Promising me a place in the annals of martial art history. But, do a search on Hapkido or Taekwondo history, or the techniques of these arts, and Scott Shaw or scottshaw.com in nowhere to be found.

Maybe one of you web experts have an answer to all of this. I do not.

In closing, I think this is an ideal example of life. We each live in our moment. We each live it for a time… But, then our moment will be gone. That does not mean that our moment was not lived and experienced. It just means that the all of the everything out there is in a constant state of flux. It is ever-changing. We are here. Then, we are gone.

Think about it… What happens when the internet forgets you?

*　*　*

28/Aug/2025 07:39 AM

Most conversations you have today will be forgotten by tomorrow.

Most happiness you feel today will be forgotten by tomorrow.

Most sadness you feel today will be forgotten by tomorrow.

Most anger you feel today will be forgotten by tomorrow.

Most people of the world could care less what you think or feel; if you are happy, sad, angry, or anything else.

Meaning, no matter how much something matters to you, it matters to no one else.

What does that tell you about how you should live your life?

GUNS OF EL CHUPACABRA, GOOGLE, AND, YOU NEVER HAVE TRUE POWER OVER YOURSELF
27/Aug/2025 06:55 AM

A few days back, someone hit me up and said that the main page for the Zen Film, *Guns of El Chupacabra,* on my website, was not coming up in the main search at Goggle. Okay… It has been coming up for like two decades, (or more), but… So me, I popped the search, just to check it out. And yes, the guy was right. The main page—the, *"Official Webpage,"* for *Guns of El Chupacabra* was no longer coming up in the Google search. This, though other pages on my website, regarding the Zen Film were listed???

Why this??? How did this happen? I have no idea. Maybe you do??? I hope that you do. Tell me. Fix it!

I did all that I can do in the Google Search Console, as the proprietor of the website, scottshaw.com. In addition, I checked the host, the server, the SEO and all that good stuff. They're all good. Plus, the page is listed and fed from a lot of outside sources. But, it is still not coming up in the Google search.

Many/most of the webpages devoted to my other Zen Films on the site come up. So, what happened? I do not know what or why?

I know there is this guy in my feed on the socials who gives all kind of tips on how to make your site or your page move up in the Google search. I have listened and learn a lot. But, as I am not trying to sell anything—I do not run a on-line business, or anything like that. And, as the search for my films are so specific, I don't have a lot of search competition. Thus, his information is interesting but not all that useful, at least not for me. And, if the main page devoted to a film is not in play, what's up?

I guess this all goes to the reality of life… How much control do you actually have over your life. I mean, there are all these/those external influences in play that you have no control over. You live your life as best as you can, but then something unexpected hits. Then what? What can you do? I do not know???

So, if any of you people out there who are web wizards, and you can help me, go for it. Thanks in advance! If not, just understand that Google is not the ultimate truth of the ultimate truth. Sometimes, it gets it wrong. And then, (when it does)... ...Really... Then, what???

Just know that the truth of the truth is hiding there within the individual. And, if someone else hides it from you, that does not mean that it does not exist. You may just have to search a little bit harder to find it.

DREAM YOGA: EXPLORING THE PATHWAYS OF ENLIGHTENED SLEEP
26/Aug/2025 01:34 PM

Dream Yoga is an ancient spiritual practice rooted in Tibetan Buddhism, specifically within the tradition of the Kagyu and Nyingma schools. Its purpose is to cultivate awareness within the dream state, transforming ordinary dreams into an active field for spiritual growth, self-realization, and insight. Unlike Western lucid dreaming practices, which often focus on psychological exploration, Dream Yoga is deeply interwoven with Buddhist philosophy and the pursuit of enlightenment.

The Origins of Dream Yoga

Dream Yoga finds its origins in the teachings of the legendary Indian Buddhist Master Padmasambhava, also known as, Guru Rinpoche. Rinpoche brought these esoteric practices to Tibet in the eighth century. The yogic exploration of dreams is documented in the, *"Six Yogas of Naropa,"* a set of advanced tantric practices for accomplished meditators. Tibetan monks and yogis have, for centuries, used Dream Yoga as a method for understanding the illusory nature of existence and for gaining direct insight into the workings of the mind.

The Philosophy Behind Dream Yoga

At its core, Dream Yoga is founded upon the notion that life itself is like a dream—transient, insubstantial, and ever-changing. Buddhist philosophers argue that our waking reality and our dream reality are fundamentally similar in their lack of inherent solidity. By realizing the dreamlike nature of all phenomena, practitioners of Dream Yoga aim to cultivate non-attachment, compassion, and wisdom.

Dream Yoga teaches that consciousness is not bound to the physical body and can be developed and freed through meditative practice, both awake and asleep. The ultimate goal is to recognize the emptiness and luminous clarity of mind—the realization that all experiences, whether waking or dreaming, are projections of consciousness.

Distinguishing Dream Yoga from Lucid Dreaming

Dream Yoga and lucid dreaming share the basic principle of becoming aware within a dream. However, their intention and methodology sets them apart. Lucid dreaming, as commonly practiced in the West, typically aims at personal exploration, creativity, or overcoming nightmares. Dream Yoga, in contrast, is primarily a spiritual discipline intended to extend meditative awareness into sleep, thereby deepening insight and progressing on the path to enlightenment.

In Dream Yoga, lucidity is just the beginning. Once lucidity is achieved, practitioners employ a set of advanced techniques to manipulate, dissolve, and ultimately transcend dream phenomena. The focus shifts from controlling the dream environment to realizing the dream's illusory nature and using this realization to inform one's waking life.

The Stages of Dream Yoga

1. Cultivating Lucidity

The first stage of Dream Yoga is to become aware that one is dreaming. This is practiced through a combination of daytime mindfulness and nighttime affirmations. Practitioners train themselves to question reality throughout the day with phrases like, *"Am I dreaming?"* This habit is designed to carry over into sleep, triggering lucidity.

Other techniques include keeping a dream journal to enhance dream recall, performing reality checks, and setting intentions before sleep. In Tibetan traditions, certain visualizations, mantras, and breathing exercises are also used to prime the mind for lucidity.

2. Stabilizing Lucidity

Once inside a lucid dream, the practitioner must stabilize the experience. This involves grounding oneself in the dream by focusing on details, rubbing the hands together, or engaging with the dream environment. The goal is to prolong lucidity and prevent premature awakening.

3. Transforming the Dream

With stable lucidity, the practitioner begins to experiment with dream phenomena. Typical exercises include flying, passing through walls, or changing the dream scene. These acts serve not only to test the boundaries of the dream but also to confront fears, desires, and mental patterns that appear in symbolic form.

4. Recognizing the Illusion

The essence of Dream Yoga is to recognize the dream as an illusion, mirroring Buddhist teachings on the nature of reality. Practitioners meditate on the emptiness of dream objects, attempting to dissolve them or witness their transformation. The realization that even the most vivid dream is nothing more than a mental projection is a profound step toward understanding the emptiness of waking life.

5. Practicing Clear Light

Advanced practitioners of Dream Yoga may encounter what is known as the, *"Clear light,"* state—a luminous, formless awareness that arises at the deepest level of dreaming.

In Tibetan Buddhism, this Clear Light is considered the fundamental nature of mind, accessible both in sleep and at the moment of death. Training in Dream Yoga is said to prepare one for the bardo, the transitional state between death and rebirth, by fostering familiarity with the mind's luminous ground.

Practical Benefits of Dream Yoga

Practicing Dream Yoga offers a wide range of psychological, spiritual, and practical benefits: Enhanced Mindfulness: By training awareness during sleep, practitioners develop a heightened sense of mindfulness in waking life.

Overcoming Fear: Facing fears in the dream state can help dissolve anxieties and transform one's relationship to fear.

Insight into the Mind: Dream Yoga reveals the workings of subconscious patterns and conditions, offering direct insight into the mind's nature.

Preparation for Death: Tibetan Buddhism teaches that Dream Yoga prepares one for the bardo, helping to maintain awareness during the transition of death.

Spiritual Growth: The practice deepens one's understanding of emptiness, impermanence, and compassion.

Challenges and Considerations

Despite its profound benefits, Dream Yoga is not an easy practice. Achieving and maintaining lucidity requires patience, discipline, and dedication. Cultural and psychological factors may also influence one's ability to recall and engage with dreams. Some practitioners may encounter unsettling or deeply personal dream content, which can be challenging to process.

Traditional Dream Yoga is often taught under the guidance of a qualified teacher, especially within Tibetan Buddhist contexts. Independent seekers can benefit from reading texts such as, *"The Tibetan Yogas of Dream and Sleep,"* by Tenzin Wangyal Rinpoche or exploring modern resources on lucid dreaming with a spiritual focus.

Dream Yoga in Contemporary Context

While Dream Yoga remains a core practice among advanced Tibetan Buddhist yogis, its principles are increasingly being explored in the West. The intersection between scientific research on sleep and dreams, Western psychology, and Eastern spiritual traditions has given rise to a renewed interest in conscious dreaming. Many mindfulness and meditation practitioners incorporate Dream Yoga techniques into their personal development, adapting them for secular or interfaith practice.

In conclusion, Dream Yoga is a discipline that bridges the waking and dreaming worlds, offering a pathway to deeper self-awareness and spiritual realization. By learning to recognize, transform, and ultimately transcend the illusions of the dream state, practitioners illuminate the profound truth that our waking reality is equally fleeting and insubstantial. In the words of Guru Rinpoche, *"If you recognize the dream as a dream, you will awaken to the true nature of mind."*

Whether approached as a spiritual practice, a tool for personal growth, or a journey of psychological discovery, Dream Yoga invites us to explore the vast landscape of consciousness—awakening not only from our dreams, but to the dreamlike nature of reality itself.

THE WAY IT USED TO BE
25/Aug/2025 08:39 AM

For anyone who came up through a traditional system of the martial arts in the 1960s and 1970s, you will understand how different the traditional martial arts are today compared to yesterday. Back then, it was very intense, as much of the training was at least marginally full-contact. It was not unusual to come home from a class bruised and battered. I know I did.

Even in a system like my main focus of the time, Hapkido, where there is a lot of throwing involved; those throws could become very extreme.

Back when I was a twelve or thirteen years old, I had this one instructor, who, for whatever reason, decided I was the perfect patsy. He would toss my ass through the air at virtually every class. Which, as I trained daily, was every day. Even some of the other students wondered, and would ask me, why I was always the fall guy. I had no answer. But, I truly learned what taking a fall felt like from that style of training.

I've never spoken too much about this instructor, as I only spend maybe a year with him. He was a Chinese-American man, who had progressed up to the third-degree black belt, which was a very high rank at that time. He had been trained here in the United States, under the direction of one of the first Hapkido practitioners to come to America. Plus, he held a black belt in Judo. So, he knew his stuff. The thing was, he was very old-school in his training methods. He mostly worked with Hapkido hand-techniques and the throws, teaching only the most basic of kicking techniques. But, what he taught was intense.

Like many instructors of the era, he would sit at his desk by the big windows of his studio, smoking his cigarettes, and hoping for new students to join his school. Of which, there were many.

I actually learned a lot from that man and his method of teaching. Techniques and ideas that have stayed with me to this day. My reason for leaving his school was much the same as most of the advanced students who moved on. We wanted to stay closer to the source, so we only desired to train with Korean-born, first-generation instructors.

After my time with him, I bounced around to a few different schools, just to stay in the game, and keep my learning curve moving up. I did this until I met an instructor in Korea, who came to America, and we operated a couple schools.

The thing that I have witnessed, through the years, with each new generation of instructor moving farther and farther away from the source of the various traditional systems of martial arts, is how the training has diminished and become, for lack of a better term, softer.

I get it. Times changed and you no longer can send your students home with a bruised-up body and/or even some broken bones. I can't even remember how many bones I've broken via training. But, that was then. This became now.

Certainly, with the introduction of first Full-Contact Kickboxing, then Brazilian Jujitsu and MMA, again training was taking to the level of, *"Hurt,"* orientated. But, this is not the case with the traditional forms of the martial arts. They have, at least seemingly, been diminished. This is ideally illustrated with a system like traditional Taekwondo. Once a fully actualized system of self-defense, which later moved towards being solely sport orientated, with an ever-increasing level of limited techniques.

I believe this becomes a question of life/in life, is change and evolution always a good thing? Or, with change is something lost in the essence of the original?

This is just something to think about for you marital artists out there and for the everybody else, as well. Does change always make things better? Or, is change simply change? And with change, is something always gained or is something always lost?

THE POLITICS OF JOY
25/Aug/2025 06:41 AM

How happy are you in your life? How much joy do you feel? How much time do you spend in a state of bliss? Or, how much time do you spend doing just the opposite?

Most people as they pass through their life simply exist. Sure, every now and then, when they get something they want or something is going their way, they get happy. But, they do not spend their life in a condition of joy.

The fact is, many religions and a lot of general people at large tell an individual to steer away from embracing and cultivating the feeling of joy. They explain that it is not good or not holy or not whatever. They exclaim that they should instead only seek a calm and steady life, solely focused on working on the life essential.

Again, how about you? How have you been instructed and taught to feel in terms of happiness and joy? And, how often do you even think about this subject.

In New Age Circles, a few decades past, it was a time when people were told to embrace the joy. ...To seek it out and to live it to its fullest. Terms like, *"Peak Experience,"* were used to guide people into embracing that enhanced sense of ecstasy.

All that seems gone now. But, that does not mean that it is no longer possible.

I have watched presentations where neuroscientists scan individual's brains, and they found that certain people have certain elements that simply cause them to feel more joy than others. If you're one of those people, good for you! I believe my wife is. I'm always envious, in that abstract sort of way, as I seem to be just the opposite. Well, when my mother was pregnant with me, she would later often brag that all she did was drink coffee and smoke and from that no one even knew she was pregnant. So, (I guess), I did not have the best incubator to rise up into life. But, you can't change what you can't change. All you are left with is all you are left with.

But, what it all really comes down to is what you choose to do with your life, how you choose to live it, and how you choose to feel. How do you choose to feel? Do you just want to live life defined by all that is going on around you—all that you cannot control. Or, do you choose to take a step towards embracing a consciousness of joy?

From my experience, the best way to do it is to simply do it. We all know what joy feels like. At least I hope we all know that feeling. So, just do it!

In fact, right now, stop the reading, and start the feeling. Simply let the sensation of joy enter your being. Bring it into your being. Instigate and become that emotion.

I'M SORRY, MEANS NOTHING
23/Aug/2025 07:04 AM

What do you do when you do something that hurts someone else? What do you do to fix or repair what you have done? More importantly, why did you do what you did in the first place?

In life, we are all going to have things happen to us that we wish did not occurred. That's just life. Many of those things will be brought on by someone else.

Here is where the complexities of life come into play. Most of these incidents can be chalked up to accidents. The person who did what they did, did not really mean to do what they did to you. In other cases, however, sometimes people do things to intentionally hurt someone else. Of course, there are a million reasons for each action a person takes, but at the core of their being, I always question, *"What kind of individual would intentionally do anything that hurts anyone?"* Yet, those occurrences do happen.

In your own life, have you ever hurt someone intentionally? If you truly chart your way through that life incidents, isn't that a wrong thing to have done? What did it prove? That you have the power to hurt someone? If that is your life goal, don't you think that desire should be reevaluated?

In your own life, have you ever hurt someone unintentionally? If you have, what did you do after that fact?

I know, throughout the many years of my own life, some people have hurt me. A few have even done what they did intentionally. Though I may have even understand their motivations, from a philosophic level, don't you think it is only the lowest level of human being that would hurt anyone deliberately, no matter what their motivation?

Basically, hurting someone intentionally is based upon desire. Desire for power, desire for retribution, desire to hurt, desire for desire. Have you ever done that? And, what was the ultimate outcome? Yes, maybe you got over on that person. Yes, maybe you received what you wanted in that moment. But, in the long run of your life, what did it cost you? Most will find, once they have lived farther down their road of life, that what they did ultimately affected them negatively, and brought negative karma their direction, and ultimately a life that did not become all that it could have become.

On the other side of this issue, and the more common pattern of life, is that much of the time, when hurt or pain, or whatever other undesired act is instigated, it is done by accident. Though some would say, *"There is no such thing as an accident."* And, essentially that is most likely true. Nonetheless, what was done was not done with the intent to hurt. Then what?

What do you do when you have hurt someone, in some way, whether intentionally or not? What do you do to try to fix it?

Most likely, if you truly are a good human being, and you do actually care about life and humanity and all that is good and right, the first place you go to is to say, *"I'm sorry."* I know that is my first means of apology. But, what does, *"I'm sorry,"* really mean? And, perhaps, better put, what does it accomplish? Yes, it is owning your responsibility in your action. But, what does it change? What can it change? And, if you do not do something to actually undo what you have done; whatever you have done—whatever damage you have created, lives on forever. Do you ever think about that? Do you even care?

I know myself, whenever I have done something to hurt someone, I feel terrible about it. I am just one of those people who possess the makeup to feel really terrible and hold a lot of guilt about that kind of stuff. But, feeling bad or guilty doesn't change the action. Only action changes the action. And, this is where I believe many people fall short in life. When they have instigated something that has done damage to the life of someone else, even if they do say, *"I'm sorry,"* that is where it ends. They do nothing to undo or fix what they have unleashed. And, I get it, sometimes what you have done to hurt that someone else is not easy to fix. But, if you do not put a very conscious effort into trying, that means, you saying, *"I'm sorry,"* has no true meaning.

So, think about all of this the next time you hurt someone. Think about all of this next time someone hurts you. Saying, *"I'm sorry,"* means nothing, unless action is taken to fix what you/what they have done. Can you put your ego and your desires and all of that kind of negative stuff away and actually do what it takes to truly fix the hurt you've created?

If you can, good for you. If you can't, what does that say about you?

ARE YOU HATIN' OR ARE YOU CREATIN'
22/Aug/2025 09:04 AM

Life is a process of what you do. Your life is defined by what you do. What you do or do not do becomes the ultimate definition of your life.

Think about something you hoped to do when you were younger. We all had a certain fantasy of what we saw our life evolving into when we were in our youth. What was yours? Did you follow that path? Did you try to become? Or, did you get sidetracked?

If you did follow that path, where did it lead you? No matter where you ultimately ended up, did not the process of pursuing that dream at least provide you with a lot of life experiences that you call up from your memory?

If you did not pursue chasing that life path, and all you did was to allow yourself to be lost in fantasy, taking no true action toward actualizing your one-time dream, where has your life lead you? What did you lose by not following that dream? And, somewhere deep inside, do you not still wish you could have done something more about who your ultimate became?

When a person is young, they possess a sense of forever. There will always be time to chase that dream. The problem is, time is an evil master, everyone gets old.

A very important thing to do, no matter where you find yourself in life, is to look to the life of those people who are older that you—those who have lived their life, pursuing whatever path they choose to follow. It is truly from them that you can learn a lot about those who never followed their dream. This is also the case, and the ultimate definition of a person's life, when they die. Who were they when they died? What have they left behind?

Some people spend their entire existence looking to and living their life via the life of other people. Whether that is loving or hating a sports team, the people at their job, or looking to the life of other people, and what they have created or achieved, as means of driving their emotions, leading to their assessments of that other person or other something, ultimately providing them with a false sense of sustenance for their own reality. The thing is, living your life defined by the life of someone else, equals nothing in the realm of what you, personally, have achieved.

Truly, where are you in the pursuit of your dreams? Your dreams of today and/or your dreams of yesterday?

Certainly, many of us, when we were young, held the dream of massive achievement. And, some did achieve that status. But, the reality of the reality is, most of us will never meet that goal. But, the goal we can achieve is the purposely turning off all levels of negativity in our life, stopping all they things that bring unhappiness or harm to anyone or anything, and set about on a path of actually positively doing what we hoped to do.

How about you? Where do you find yourself in this process? Are you still trying to live that dream? Or, have you given up?

Every day of your life you have the chance to make a choice about what it is you are going to do. What are you going to do?

Every day of your life you have the change to follow your dream. There is never a guarantee that you will achieve your ultimate fantasy. But, there is a one-hundred percent chance that you can try.

For anyone who has arrived at adulthood, we each understand that we must take on responsibilities to put a roof over our head and take care of our family and loved ones. This being said, there is always Free Time.

What do you do with your Free Time? Do you spend it spacing out, throwing some or all of your energy into what someone else is doing or has achieved? Or, do you spend it pursing your dream?

Your life, your choice.

        *   *   *

21/Aug/2025 06:54 AM

The ultimate definition of your life comes down to one thing, the worst thing that you've done.

Most people live in denial about what they've done.

Most people try to hide what they've done.

Most people try to hide from what they've done.

But, what you have done is what you have done and that is your ultimate definition.

*   *   *

20/Aug/2025 07:14 AM

When was the last time you got mad at god?

WHAT'S ON THE HEADSTOCK
19/Aug/2025 06:55 AM

I've recently been pushed into thinking a lot about the brand and the name of a guitar and what it really means...

Let's step back a few decades to begin this discussion.

By the late 1970s, and through the 1980s, guitar customization was the name of the game. Particularly with electric guitars. People would have coil splitters and phase switches added to the pickup electronics on their guitar. All kinds of pickup changing and replacing; adding and removing of pickups and various other configurations was taking place. I thought it was a really fun time as music was still in its analog stage and getting new sounds, by these various methods, was an adventure.

Hand-in-hand with this era came the fact that a lot of luthiers were creating guitars and guitar parts for their clients. My friend, Jim Foote did all kinds of crazy stuff for me back in the day. I remember on this one birthday he ever gave me a guitar he had made for me. Very cool! Thanks!

At least in the field of rock music, the Stratocaster style guitar was king. If you look at music videos from that era, you will notice that there are names, other than the most known of say, *"Fender,"* becoming obvious on the headstocks of many guitars. Plus, as a lot of luthiers made specialized necks for the guitar bodies of their clients, many a guitar and no name on the headstock at all.

Some guitars were made from scratch, as well. For example, my friend Kris Derrig made what has become probably one of the most famous, *"Replica,"* guitars ever created. He made a 1959 Gibson Les Paul, with the actual, *"Gibson,"* logo on the headstock, of which Slash ended up with, and used it to record some of the music on the seminal Guns and Roses album, *Appetite for Destruction.* Kris unfortunately passed away way too young in life, at the age of only thirty-two, and never got to know about or experience any of the success of his name or his guitars. But, I won't speak of that right now. You can read the piece I have about him and his guitars on this website, if you feel like it.

Anyway... And, to the point of this piece... The guitars he made were not true Gibson Les Pauls. Some people, at least back then, would call them, *"Fakes."* And, I guess they were. Had people like Slash and Lenny Kravitz and Charlie Daniels not used them, he and the guitars he made may have faded away in history with no mention.

The thing is, there are a number of people who are at that level of luthier craftsmanship, like my aforementioned friend, Jim Foote, (who Kris worked for), and they can make excellent reproductions. And, many have throughout the years. In fact, when a craftsman is putting the energy into make one guitar at a time, they are oftentimes much better than a factory-made instrument. But, that does not mean they become a true Gibson simply because someone puts a Gibson logo on the headstock.

The few guitars that Kris made during his lifetime have gained astronomical value. But, again, though they the Gibson name on the headstock, they are not a Gibson. So, what are they?

I was driven to thinking about all of this via my nephew, who I have come to be very impressed with. I have mentioned him in this blog before. He is still a young teenager, yet he already has created a lot of music, and he got it out there on the music services. He is now moving away from keyboards and onto electric guitar. His mother, (obviously), came to me to see if I had a guitar to give him, as he is currently borrowing a Charvel from her boyfriend. This put me in a bit of a pickle, however. What guitar should I give him??? She doesn't want it to be too high-end, as she puts it, *"He's just a beginner."* But, I don't want to give him a piece of junk.

This caused me to go over to my studio and go through my collection. You know, I am certainly no luthier, but through my many decades of playing, I have gained a certain, (minor), skillset in guitar repair and construction. I was looking through a few Strat style guitars I have put together, throughout the years, with, as mentioned, necks that came from various sources. A couple of them, I put a logo on that says, *"Fucker Stratocaster."*

There was this guy on Esty a few years back that was selling that decal. I thought it was pretty funny. So, I grabbed a few.

I jokingly suggested to my lady that I give him one of those, *"You can't do that! He takes the guitar to school,"* she exclaims.

I also looked through a few guitars that I had put a Fender Stratocaster decal on the headstock and then strayed lacquer over it. They look original. But, they are not.

Some of those guitars are really good players. But, times have changed since the 80s, and things that aren't the Real Deal, aren't the Real Deal. I mean, everyone isn't slapping decals and logos on headstocks anymore. Well, maybe some people are. But...

Certainly, all of the fake Gibsons coming out of China have overwhelmed the market. Some of which are pretty good guitars, however. But, again, I couldn't give him one of those...

So, I was stuck. What to do? His mother doesn't want be to give him a high-dollar instrument and I can't give him one of my guitars, created for my very specific specifications. Answer: I ended up buying him a guitar from a respected brand at Guitar Center. I ordered it online. Throw in a nice practice amp and they'll be here in a few day... The guitar, it's real. It's good. It's not super high-end. I guess that checks all the boxes???

But, what does all of this mean to you and why am I boring you with all of this nonsense?

Ask yourself, *"What is real?"* I mean, really, *"What is real?"* Particularly on the internet and on the opinionated news networks, I hear so many people saying so many things that just are not true. They base their speak on some reality conjured up only in their own opinionated mind, based upon opinions with little or no foundations. Yet, it is said and it is believed.

Just like a Kris Derrig Les Pual with a Gibson logo… Was it a better constructed guitar than one that came out of the Gibson factory? Maybe. Does the logo you or I put on a Strat make it a true Fender or just a Fucker?

Everything is deceiving. Looks are deceiving. …As the old saying goes. So, what is real? And, if it is real, does that mean that it is necessarily better? I don't know??? What do you think?

Real or Fake, it is a very fine line.

* * *
18/Aug/2025 11:01 PM

When all your memories are forgotten who will remember them?

YOU ARE WHAT YOU EAT
18/Aug/2025 07:32 AM

I was leaving this one restaurant that I frequent, after having breakfast—going out the back door towards their parking lot. I noticed that this one waitress who works there, who is very nice, was standing by the kitchen eating her breakfast. What was she eating? Flamin' Hot Cheetos and a Mountain Dew.

Wow, I thought, how strange. One of the main reasons I like this restaurant is that they serve a number of really healthy dishes. And, I know, the employees can eat there for free. Why does she choose to eat that garbage?

Don't get me wrong... I don't mean to be judgmental here. Because we all have our vices that other people may question or may not like. But, it just seems that the problems consuming bad foods, on a regular basis can cause, are not good. And, Mountain Dew, we all have heard the stories about the side-effects of that. Like the old saying goes, *"You are what you eat."*

I mean, me, I haven't consumed a soft drink in years. A lot of years... I only drink them when it is an absolute necessity. Even most fast food places offer bottled water now.

This young lady is very nice. She's actually a singer in band. I didn't know that for a long-long time until recently she told me. I looked up her band and she, the shinning element of the group, is a very good singer. I think the problem with the band, if you want to call it that, is that they are all much older than her. Maybe one of the members is her man, or something? I don't know??? But, here in a place like L.A., with a million other bands on the market, I think the age of the rest of her group really holds her back. But, such is life. And, that's the not the point of this piece anyway.

What you consume defines who and what you are. Sure, you can do it, hiding out in the parking lot in the back of the business, but you're still doing it. You're still taking it in. And, whatever you consume will ultimately come to define your life.

What do you eat? What do you drink? Why do you eat it and why do you drink it? What else do you consume? And, most importantly, how does it define your life today and how will it define your life tomorrow? If you don't think about this, you really should. Because if you do not intake what you intake with absolute consciousness, it may be the source your eventually downfall.

HOW HOLLYWOOD FORGETS YOU
17/Aug/2025 07:20 AM

Certainly, I can say, that Don Jackson, (Donald G. Jackson), was the first filmmaker to make me a star. As I have stated in way too many places to mention, though he may not have been the first individual who put me in the first position of a film, he was definitely the first person to put me in the lead position of a film that has stood the test of time.

This is not to say, that it did not come with a cost. I had entered the film game about a year before I met him, and I had done pretty well… I was moving up the ladder.

Recently, I saw an interview with Brad Pitt and Leonardo DiCaprio. Pitt was speaking about how he was an extra in a film and tried to say something in the scene, but the AD stopped him. DiCaprio didn't get it. …DiCaprio, who I actually knew as a young child, as he and his mother lived next-door to my best friend in Hollywood. He came into the game early and successfully, working his way up the ladder from childhood. Pitt, had to fight his way to stardom as an adult.

The thing is, that was the only way to get your SAG, (Screen Actors Guild), card back in the day. And, a SAG card was and is the only way to be a real actor. …The only way to get your SAG card was to have a line in an actual film.

Me, pretty much the moment I got into the game, I was cast in a small role in the film, *The Bonfire of the Vanities*. I said something to Bruce Willis. Bruce Willis… So sad what has become of his life. But, he can rest on the fact that he has made some incredible films. My moment of speaking was cut from the final version of that film, but nonetheless, I still had become a, *"Real,"* actor with a SAG card.

I was on the way to becoming a working actor in the A-game. Then, I met DGJ.

The problem is, once you dip your feet in the B-Market, at least back then, it is very hard to ever reemerge. The industry defined you as a, *"Something,"* and that was that. You're A-Market career is over. Even Don knew this fact. And, I believe, he felt a certain sense of guilt about what he had done to my up-and-coming career, as every now and then he would say something to me and other people about this fact.

In any case, he made me the lead. Now/Then, as stated, this was not the first time I had been in that spot. A few people had come my direction, prior to this—believing in me. But, for better or for worse—for whatever stupid karmic reason, I choose to walk the path with Don.

I so remember this one moment... We were in Hollywood shooting a scene for *The Roller Blade Seven,* and it was all about me. The camera was on me, and only me. I had this realization of just how special that moment was. A moment that I hoped would last forever.

As I evolved in my filmmaking career, I provided a number of people with that same chance. Some in front of the camera and some behind. How many appreciated that? I don't know? I know a lot didn't give a damn, believing they deserved it. But where are they now? Did they ever go on to do anything else that was meaningful? Answer: No.

What I am saying here is that, when opportunity comes knocking, you've got to take it. You've got to take it because, though you may have all of these vivid dreams about what you hope to become, none of that stuff may ever happen. If you do not take what is offered to you, and you do not live it to the fullest, you may never be presented with that opportunity again.

WAY TOO FORGIVING
16/Aug/2025 01:19 PM

The last time I was in Hong Kong, I was standing on a streetcorner, waiting for the light to change, to cross the street. It did. As I got to the other side, I noticed that there was a young lady, looking at her phone. BAM, this guy bumps into her very hard and her phone goes smashing to the ground. She picks it up and I could tell (at least) the screen was broken. The guy kept walking not giving the incident a second thought. The young lady stood there staring at her broken phone and watching the guy walk off into the distance. I thought that was pretty fucked up.

You know, every now and then, I tell you stories about my life and my life interactions with people that are not all that appealing. At least not appeal to me as someone else is doing some fucked up something to me. But me, I always try to take the high road in these situations. As those of you who have been reading this blog awhile, you certainly understand this to be true.

I forget what stories I have actually mentioned. I know one of them was a year or two ago when this lady had obviously rescued a dog from a shelter. For whatever reason that dog hated men. I would see her walking the dog, on a daily basis, and the dog was always growling at men that he passed.

Me, one day, I had no choice but to walk past the woman, who was standing on the side of the sidewalk with her German Shepard. As I approached, the dog started really freaking out. But, my thought process was, animals always love me. Then, he broke loose from her grip and jumped at me. Just as I was about to defend myself, he knocked me over this knee level city water structure thing that I didn't realize was right behind me. I flew onto my back on the ground. The dog didn't bite me, but just sniffed me. *"Get this fucking dog off of me!"* I was pissed; obviously. When I got to my feet, I was about to call the cops but then I realized, was it really the dog's fault? If I did call them, they would probably put him down. And, I love animals. I would not want to be responsible for that. So, I just angrily walked away.

I don't know if I mentioned this one to you??? But, a few weeks ago, I was taking a walk with my lady one afternoon. Passing a supermarket, this way too old to drive man barrels out, not even looking, and runs over my right foot, just as we were passing the driveway to the store. I smash my hand into the rear window of the SUV. *"You fucking ran over my foot!"* But, he just drove on. That was hit and run. I could have called the cops. But, what good is that going to do? I could have sued him. But... That is just not the person I am.

To bring all of this up to today. Well actually, yesterday... A couple of weeks ago, this young African-American guy, who delivers the newspaper, (remember those), to people around my neighbor was driving. I was turning left and he was going straight. He didn't stop at the stop sign and BANG, our cars hit. It was very minor, but we exchanged information and all of that. Seemed like a nice enough guy. He lived in Compton.

Anyway... I reported it to my insurance company. I took my car to the shop. They had it all fixed up, good as new, in about a week. No problem. Not fun. But, not the end of the world. I thought it was all over.

Then... Yesterday... I get a letter from his insurance company telling me the accident was completely my fault. Are you kidding me! He shot the stop sign!

I thought the guy would be honest and man-up. Tell the truth. He seemed like a good dude.

I played it all down to my insurance company, and to his, so it would not hurt his standing. I thought I was doing the right thing. Helping him out. I guess that's what being a nice guy gets you.

Because of all of this, I had to go and take a photo of the stop sign that he ran, where the accident occurred. I emailed it to my insurance company and to his insurance company. And now, I suppose, I am going to have to deal with it all over again. Something I just do not want to do!

Just stupid!!! A waste of time, emotions, and energy.

So, here we are in this world. Is it the right thing to go after anyone/everyone who hurts you, to whatever degree, large or small, no matter what? Or, is it better to be forgiving? I always fight with that question. I mean, a lot of people have fucked me over throughout my life. Even people I have gone out of my way to help. But, like I always say, hurt only equals hurt, and hurt is never good.

As stated, I always try to take the high road. ...To be forgiving... But, when you do, like this latest life incident, sometimes it is you who gets fucked over in the process.

Tell me, what is the answer?

* * *

15/Aug/2025 02:03 PM

Quoting a lie does not make it the truth.

CLEANING UP YOUR LIFE
15/Aug/2025 07:11 AM

As it says in the Tao Te Ching, *"To the person of the world, everyday something is gained. To the person of Tao, everyday something is lost."*

These few words are very profound and are a simple, yet ideal, guideline for how one can emerge into becoming the best representation of themselves.

These words also depict a clear representation of the mindset possessed in Zen. By following the path of least resistance, while removing as many desires and, thus, obstacles from your life as possible, you will emerge into a clearer state of understanding.

Think about your own life. Think about the things that you do on a daily basis. Look into your mind. What desires are you bound by? Look around your life, how have the possessions you own helped your existence and how have they hindered your reality? What did the process of obtaining them do to your reality, then, now, and beyond?

Most people do very specific things each day of their life. The foods, the drinks, and the substances they intake come to define who they are, what they become, and how they will eventually die. They define how they interact with the world around them. What they do to earn a living is also the same. What they do as a means to make a living, and what they do in their spare time all contribute to the karma they create, not only for themselves but for all of those who are close to them and beyond. Yet, most people never question any of this, they simply do. But, in that doing, birth, creation, and their ultimate demise are all set into motion.

Stop right now. What do you do on a daily basis that does not contribute to a pure mind and a more purified living space for yourself and all of those around you? What have you created in your life, the life of those you love, and the greater world as a whole by what you are doing and what you have done?

If you do not think about this on a daily basis, don't you believe that you should?

The problem is, most people never take the time to question, study, and then very consciously form their own reality. They are simply cast to whatever life hands them, defined by what they like and/or do not like. They never study how what they do not only affects the ultimate outcome of their life but the life of all those around them. How about you?

The things is, you can live a more clear, more pure, and more actualized life, if you choose to. The question is, do you choose to? Are you willing to remove all of things that remove the purity from your life and enter into a space of conscience refinement? The fact is, all choices that lead to any life of betterment must be made by you. They must a conscience choice leading to conscience action. They cannot be forced on you. What choice to do you make?

Ultimately, your life comes down to what you plan to do with it. The definition of your life comes down to what you have done to others.

What have you lived? What have you done? What are you living? What are you doing? Is what you are living and what you are doing making you a better, more pure, and more enlightened individual? Or, is what you are doing casting your shadows of unenlightened behavior out and onto all those you know and all of those who come into contact with you?

As is always the case, your life is your choice. What are you going to do with that choice; live a life defined by purity and refined consciousness or not?

THE FORGOTTEN MASTERS
13/Aug/2025 11:25 AM

For anyone who had the privilege of studying a traditional form of the martial arts under the direction of an Asian-born instructor who came to the West directly from the country where that system of self-defense had its origin, you will understand that what is taught to the students directly under the guidance of an instructor with that foundation is quite different from what a student learns who is taught by a second or a third or a fourth generation teacher, of Western origins, that came to learn the art in some other country than where it originated. This is not necessary to say that these instructors are lesser practitioners of the art. What it does imply, however, is that something is lost with each generation of practitioners who has not studied their system of self-defense directly from a teacher who was trained in the country of its origin.

For those of us who have been lucky enough to train with teachers who were the first-generation instructors of the Korean martial arts, it is very easy to see the difference between how we were taught and how the newer students are now instructed. Not only have the arts evolved, which some would claim is a very good thing, but business models have largely come into play, causing much of the true origins of the arts to be convoluted with the need to make as much money as possible.

I must be clear at this point of this discussion, I am not saying that all of the teachers who moved to the West were and are honest and true individuals. Many of the first-generation students of, particularly the Korean martial arts, have found this out the hard way. Myself included. What I am saying is that there is a direct link to the deeper truths and understandings that are possessed by the people who have studied a system of martial arts directly at its point of origin than those who have only studied from an instructor who is more distantly removed from the origin of the art.

More than simply the fact that there have been many a student who was allowed to study under the guidance of these direct practitioners of the art, the fact that is missed by so many is how many of these instructors have been completely forgotten by the hands of time?

If you look to the list of immigrant-instructors of the martial arts in the United States, for example, you will see that the wider formalized teaching to Western students began to rapidly grow in the late 1940s and into the 1950s. This was first formalized by the partitioners of particularly Judo and then later Karate. By the 1960s, instructors of the then newly developed Korean martial arts began to immigrate to the United States and open up schools of self-defense. For a time, by the 1970s and into the 1980s, there was a vast number of instructors opening schools and teaching the Korean martial arts. Where have all of these instructors gone?

Certainly, as time progresses, people become older and cannot perform the physical activities of their youth as well as they once did. Others, simply passed away. Some were driven away from teaching by a changing economic landscape. But, the fact of the matter is, think about the number of instructors, who were considered to be very good, advanced practitioners of the various arts, that have all but been forgotten. There was never a newspaper or magazine article written about them. They never appeared on TV. All they did was to teach a group of students who were allowed to learn valuable life lessons from their teacher. But, now their teacher is gone. Forgotten by history.

I know from my personal perspective, some of my teachers, that I consider to be a true influence to the martial artists I became, have been completely forgotten. Look for information about them on the internet, and there is none. Yet, once upon a time, they were a respected practitioner of the art. They were invited to all of the events the advanced practitioners attended. They were at the forefront of spreading their system of marital arts to the wider audience across the globe. Now, they are forgotten.

From one perspective, being forgotten by the larger masses is not such a bad thing. They achieved what they set out to do and that was to teach as many students as possible their system of self-defense. For each of those students, and those who became instructors under their direction, their legacy lives on. On the other hand, however, I believe it is essential that we never forget those practitioners who laid the foundations for the modern martial arts. Though their name may be lost to the hands of time, what they provided, to the ever-evolving landscape of the martial arts, should never be forgotten.

* * *
13/Aug/2025 07:09 AM

You're either looking for someone to love or you're looking for someone to hate. Life is as simple as that.

HELLO KITTY GOTH
12/Aug/2025 08:21 AM

For those of you who may not know, in Japan, there is this who Hello Kitty Goth Subculture. Mostly, defined by young ladies who dress up with their interpretation of Goth clothing and hairstyles, but embrace this subculture with an emphasis on Hello Kitty. I Love it!

It has been going on for quite a long time now. I don't know exactly how long, but it's been years.

If you are walking around Harajuku, you can usually see a few young ladies dressed in this style. Or, in Ginza on the weekends, when the street is shut down to traffic. And other places, particularly around Tokyo…

The other day this one lady who embraces the Goth lifestyle, based out of Austin, was presenting some of her content. She was showing this lady around her place, and she stated, *"I didn't want her to think I was a Hello Kitty Goth."*

The thing was, she was showing off all of her very dark and, in my mind, demonic collection of things. You know, like old, petrified rats, and human bones, and actual human skulls, and the like. I mean really dark shit. I just don't like that kind of stuff.

I remember there used to be this reality show, based around this shop in the Haight, in San Francisco, where the owners and staff would go around a collect all of that kind of stuff and then sell it in their shop. I visited that shop a few times, but, (again), I am just not into those people and that stuff that worships and idolizes death and decay. I love life!!!

Anyway, the piece the Austin lady presented was fairly short. That's a good thing, for had it been any longer, I would have turned away and moved on. But, it did make me realizes… …Me, who's been into Goth since before it was even called Goth… I will take a Hello Kitty Goth any day over the ones who worship death and darkness. How about you?

HATE SPEECH IS NOT FREE SPEECH
12/Aug/2025 07:57 AM

How much of what you choose to listen to involves negativity? No, really... How much of what you choose to listen to and allow into your mind, via whatever media, is based in negativity?

How much negativity do you put out to the world? No, really... How much negativity do you broadcast out to the world via what you say, what you do, or what you create is based upon negativity?

The fact of life is, you can choose to be negative, or you can choose to be positive. If you choose to be negativity, no matter what your motivation, what are you creating? Answer: Negativity.

If, on the other hand, you choose to be positive, what are you creating? Answer: Positivity.

Negativity can be unleashed via many methods. Some are very obvious: yelling, screaming, criticizing, demeaning, stealing, or physically hurting. Others are more sublet; perhaps in the form of making jokes. But, at the end of whatever is done, if it is done to hurt or damage the life of any individual, then it creates one thing; negativity.

Seriously, how much negativity do you take in? And, how much negativity do you unleash?

It seems that politics creates a spark-point for a lot of negativity. Certainly, at this point in world history, there are a lot of people disliking what is going on due to the politics that surrounds them. Putin and his war on Ukraine has not only taken the lives of so many people, but has destroyed the life of a lot more. What was instigated by the attack on Israel by Hamas, which has led to Israel's scorched-earth policy towards Hamas, has killed and destroyed the life of so many people. Both of these situations are still going on as I write this, with no clearcut end in sight. It's wrong! Yet, it goes on. It was all instigated by negativity and it continues to unleash more and more negativity.

Here in the States, a lot of people seem to dislike our current president. Yes, a lot of people love him, as well. Or, he would not have been elected for a second time. But, due to all the hate, a lot of negativity is being created and unleashed. It seems that every day I get some Trump Hater in my feeds, posting hurtful things. But, does that make anything any better? No. Moreover, he is the elected president of this country; love him or hate him, that is the fact. You may wish him to not be the president. But, he is our president. If you have any patriotism, you must support our duly elected president, until you have the opportunity to elect the next one.

From a personal perspective, I know I did not like many of the policies of, *"W,"* the second Bush administration. But then, 911 happened. And, it brought this country together against a common enemy. What did that common enemy do, killed a lot of innocent people. What is that? Negativity, in its purist form. And, love our hate our president at that point in history, we all had to come together against pure negativity.

What I am suggesting here is, stop it! Stop the negativity at its source which is you. Negativity can be small or it can be very large, but the truth of negativity is that it is based upon one thing, hurtful thoughts, words, and actions.

You are the one who takes it in, and you are the one who puts it out there. Meaning, you are the one who can stop it.

At the end of the day, negativity never helps anything. If you partake of it, if you unleash it, all you are doing is hurting the world around you. Again: Stop it! Be the source of positivity. Catch negativity in is tracks and do not let it spread.

Be Positive!

YOU HAVE TO BE WILLING TO CHANGE WITH THE TIMES
11/Aug/2025 06:46 AM

So often I am confronted with people who are locked into the past. Whether this is via music, movies, the martial arts, or someone they loved way back in the way back when, they lock themselves into never changing.

But, change is good. Change is evolution. Sure, we all like what we like when we like it. But, that, *"Like,"* is never the new, the experimental, the refreshing, the evolutionary.

From the perspective of music, so often I encounter people who lock themselves into a time period of music. There is a style of music or a band or bands that they loved, most generally when they were first coming into their own, and they never move on. They are happy to listen to the same song(s) over and over and over again. But, by doing this, they trap themselves from ever evolving into the new, the more, the becoming. And, from this, they can never meet the new as the new is never presented.

In film, it is much the same. Throughout the history of cinema, there have been some great pieces of representation created. There is no doubt about that. Some people I interact with lock themselves into a period or an era or a performer, and they never move on. They watch/they experience the same performance over and over and over again. In doing this, however, they never meet the new. And, by never meeting the new, they ever meet the new. They never evolve in their vision in the what can be experienced as cinematic art.

In every moment of every decade there has been advancement in cinematic art. Filmmakers bring new visions and new ideas to the craft of filmmaking. But, for all of those who hold themselves to the expected and the known, they never allow themselves to know these new knowns. From this, no evolution is experienced.

In the world of martial arts, I frequently encounter those who locked themselves into what they are locked into. They brand themselves with the traditional systems that they were originally taught. They believe that the only true knowers were those who walked the path decades before them. ...That what was taught then was so much better than what is taught now. But, all you have to do is put one of those traditional martial artists up against one of the very-proficient MMA practitioners of today, and forget about it. They will be decimated.

The things is, times-gone-past may be beautiful. They should be respected. They laid the foundations for what we all have become today. But, yesterday is not today. And today, there is a whole new world of ideas, techniques, knowledge, and understanding, that could never have even been even contemplated yesterday.

Remember this. Yesterday was great. But, yesterday is not today. Do you want to keep yourself locked into the past? Or, do you wish to experience all of the beauty of the newly discovered today?

LOST IN THE INTERPRETATION OF YOUR REALITY
10/Aug/2025 07:40 AM

Wherever you find yourself in your life, you are defined by what you are feeling and how you are interpreting your reality. The thing is, no one else interprets your reality in the exact same manner as you. Though you may have family and friends that have lived a very similar existence as yourself, and from this, they think in a similar manner as yourself. But, they are not you. At the core of their essence, though you may agree on some or many things, their life is not your life and from this they interpret their reality different than you.

Many people project their reality onto others. They believe that due to the fact that they are thinking or feelings something in a specific manner, others should think or feel the same way, as well. Do you fall into this category?

The truth of human consciousness is, however, there is no universal definition to how anything should be interpreted. All you have to do is to remember when you lost a loved one or when something was taken from you, perhaps by theft, and from that you were caused to feel an enormous amount of emotion. Maybe someone who loved the same person or the same thing that was removed from your life was also feeling deep emotions, but they are processing those emotions in a very different manner. Step back, one of two people from this equation, and you immediately observe that with each step of distance the people care less and less. They cannot feel what you are feeling. Just as you cannot feel what they are feeling.

Some people want others to feel what they feel. They attempt to force them to feel that way. This force may take on the form of imposing guilt, strength, or even anger. But, no matter the method, the only truth of an individual who behaves in this manner is the fact that they are operating from a lower consciousness, believing that all they feel is right and justified and what others feel, if they are not feeling the exact same thing, is wrong.

The moment you understand that what you feel is only what you feel, and no one else will ever feel exactly what you are feeling, you are free. At least free to truly experience your own emotions. Though you may be one of the people who wishes to suck other people into feeling the way you feel, believing that this will give you some sort of solace, if your understand that no one will ever truly feel what you are feeling, then you allow each person to experience their own emotion and, thus, their own individual reality, from a level of their own truth. …Their own truth, and not yours.

THE IPHONE FILMMAKING SCHOOL: LESSON ONE
08/Aug/2025 09:28 AM

As I have stated, perhaps way too many times, when the nighttime gets deep and I am sitting around looking for that last grasp at inspiration sometimes I will watch music videos on the various stations that still offer such things or pop over to YouTube and let the algorithm take me where it will.

Recently, I've noticed a few music videos, created around the music of large artists, that were filmed in the elevator of the Bonaventura Hotel in DTLA. That hotel played an essential role in my life via a few pathways, but I won't speak about that here. What I will say is that, when we were filming my Zen Film, *The Rock n' Roll Cops* we did shoot at that hotel and filmed an important scene in that elevator. You can, of course, go and check out that movie on my YouTube channel, and elsewhere, if you feel like it.

Anyway, it got me to thinking… I wondered just how many takes of that scene we did, as Don was my cameraman on that film, and he was deeply lost into his obsessional camerawork at that stage of history. I even thought to maybe grab all of the footage and put it up as a collection on YouTube or something…

Yesterday, I went and dug out the footage and played it back. There were several takes and some good moments in each of them. I'm not sure which take I actually used. Or, if I used multiple takes; intercut. I mean, I edited that film so-so long ago.

But, then I decided to just let the essence of Zen remain intact and not rebroadcast the other takes of that scene. At least not right now.

One thing I did strongly come away with, from viewing that footage, was the reminder of just how easy it is to create cinematic art, if you choose to do so. I mean, there we were, my acting partner and myself. Don shooting the camera and me setting up the sound, recorded on a DAT recorder, (for the few of you out there who even know what that is), and a guy manning the sound mixer. That was it.

I don't know how big the production crew was, stuffed in that elevator for the aforementioned high-end music videos I was discussing. But, that elevator is not big. So???

The thing is, you can create art if you want to. I mean, pretty much we all like to watch movies and TV shows and music videos and all that kind of stuff we. Right? But, watching is not creating. At best, watching is veging.

Back then—back when we shot, *The Rock n' Roll Cops,* yes, film creation had become more simple. With the introduction of high-end video to the prosumer market, movies could be made for a fraction of the cost that was once necessary. Now, today, we all have our iPhone. Which, as I have, (also), stated way too many times, is a better camera with a better lens than most of the 16mm and even some of the 35mm cameras of times gone past. You can create cinematic art virtually for free. You can do it, if you choose to do it. But, do you choose to do it?

It's no secret that I have a bit of a problem with most film critics. Why? Because they never get their hands dirty and actually get out there and make a movie. It's easy to throw shade, but let's see what you can do. ...Or, they maybe make one film via a class they took or something and that's that. But, criticism is not art. Art is art. Creating art is art. And, it is now so easy to do!

A lot of times in my feeds, I get people demonstration techniques of how to film things in a creative way on an iPhone. Some of that content is very inspirational. But, if you don't do it, you don't do it. Then, what?

What I'm saying here is that art is at your fingertips. You have all the tools you need to create art right in your pocket or your purse or your backpack or your whatever.

Knowing this, what are you going to do about it? Create art, or sit back and create nothing? Your life, your choice.

TAKE A WALK BACK TO YESTERDAY
07/Aug/2025 09:46 AM

    I had popped over onto eBay this AM just to do what I do every now and then and check out and into to see if there are any of the books I'm looking for currently being offered.

    Doing a couple of searches, this one book popped up that hit this spot in me. You know, how every now and then there is that something that comes into your field of vision that causes you to go back and remember a place, a space, a time, when the world/your world was full of possibilities.

    As detailed, in times gone past, here in this blog and elsewhere, by nature, I'm really not a nostalgic person. I'm more about being here and now, then reliving or reimagining the back then. But, every now and then, it hits me too. Like it did noticing that book on eBay today.

    It sent me to a time, back in the days of Topanga Canyon, when the world was different and spirituality was raining/reigning supreme. When being spiritual actually meant something. There was this bookstore up there, back when. Every now and then, I solo, or with a friend or lover in tow, would hit it up. It was really a great bookstore. …Bookstores, remember those?

    But, like I said, spirituality was a thing back then. It meant something. And, those of us who frequented such paces, and walked the walk, had a sense of community, of belonging.

    I remember, I bought a copy of that one aforementioned book, (now on eBay), way back in the way back when at that bookstore. It was like that feeling of accomplishment. You found something that you knew would guide you in a good, new, and more positive direction. And, I believe it did.

    I thought to buy that book I saw on eBay today. But, I went and checked my shelves, and I already have a copy. See how time gets lost… See how the focus of times gone past changes. You have something, then you don't, then you do, and you don't even quite remember when you re-got it. Once, a major accomplishment. Later, just a thing.

Anyway, that/all this, does not change the fact of that feeling that seeing that book evoked. The embrace of a time when life was so much more new and so much more actualize-able.

I believe/I think we all need to embrace those moments when they come to us. Those moments where we are reminded of who we used to be. This is especially the case, when that reminded moment is of a positive nature. When we were still on the path to achieving what we hoped to become and the light at the end of the tunnel was so approachable.

THE BADNESS THAT YOU ARE
06/Aug/2025 09:23 AM

Right now, take a moment a pull up a bad quality that you have. Turn off all of your self-deception and self-denial and be extremely honest with yourself. What is it that you say, think, or do that is truly detrimental to not only your life but the life of others?

This does not have to be just one thing. Maybe there is more than one thing that defines your behavior that is not advantageous to the greater good of your life and to the life of others.

Whatever this one, (or more), things may be, clearly, right now, bring it/them into focus.

When most people hear about this exercise, they simply dismiss it. They provided all kinds of excuses to themselves, why they should not or do not need to dive deep into the who they truly are. Don't be that person! Be honest! What do you think, say, or do that is detrimental to your life and the life of others?

Once you have a definition of what that something is, bring it clearly into your mind. If you want, you can trace that action back to its source. Why have you chosen to live your life based in this behavior?

The problem with doing this, via an unfettered mind, is, however, most people will think about this for a moment or two and then their mind will begin to wander. It will be first filled with excuses and justification and then those thoughts will lead to other, undefined, unimportant thoughts, and you will become lost to a daydream. All of that helps nothing!

Instead, what you need to do is to truly isolate that part of your behavior. Really, bring it into clear mental focus. Once it is in focus, forget all of the Mind Junk that allows you to justify this action or actions. Instead, take a true look at it. How has it hurt your life? How has it hurt the life of others? Be one-hundred percent honest.

Now that you have a clear vision of this part of your personality, now that you know what it is that has created negativity in your life-sphere, what are you going to do about it? Really! What are you going to do about it?

Like most/like many people do when they encounter a dark truth about themselves, they just go into denial, stating, at best, *"That's just who I am."* Is that all you are? Do you have no control over what you have become?

The other side of this is much more proactive. Are you willing to stop doing things that not only hurt yourself and your own life evolution, but hurt the life of others?

Ultimately, are you a strong enough person to take control over your life, what you do, and how you do it? Or, are you simply out of control, dominated by your lower self, the things that happened to you in your past, and/or your inability to care about anyone or anything else, only feeding your own uncontrolled actions?

Your life is your choice. It is the choice of no one else. You have the power to define how you encounter, deal with, and live your existence. How will you live that existence? Defined by goodness, caring, and giving? Or, defined by nothing more than your lower self and the excuses you make for your actions?

THE TRUTH AS YOU WISH IT TO BE PERCEIVED
AKA HOW YOUR STORY IS TOLD
04/Aug/2025 11:26 AM

I was listening to the news on NPR, as I was driving this morning, and virtually immediately I noticed how the story being told, discussing the actions of the current administration, was so titled to one side. Plus, it was so subtle…

This is something I am always acutely aware of. …The way the news is portrayed; as it is a very subtle thing. The way the story is told, and the supporting information that is provided, can be universally balanced, or, as was the case today, it can be very tilted in one direction or the other.

I guess this should be expected. A week or so ago, the Trump administration was successful in removing all of the government funding from NPR and PBS. This has been something that the Republican Party has been attempting to do for quite some time. Finally, it has come to pass.

Wherever you land on this subject, that's not really the point of this piece. The point is, NPR and PBS have (forever) been left-leaning news services. In the past, however, there was at least a seeming attempt to bring views from both sides into their reporting. Now, apparently, the gloves are off. They will tell it the way the want to tell it, defined by their beliefs and their agenda.

The thing is, most people are never aware of this fact. …The fact that news services lean in one direction or the other, and present whatever it is they are presenting from a specific and predetermined point of view. Do you ever consider this fact? Or, do you simply believe everything you hear?

Of course, we can all say there is something very wrong in this practice. And, or course, people lean towards what they want to hear and that is where they listen or read or get whatever information it is that they are consuming.

But truly, do you ever contemplate the truth of what you are reading or hearing? Do you ever question its source? Do you ever consider that there may be another point of view—another way to present the news you are taking in? If you do, good for you! Most people are not like that, however.

I know from a personal perspective, there have been numerous times when people have attempted to tell the so-called, *"Truth,"* about Scott Shaw and my creations. But, it was wrong! Their research was very limited. Their facts were biased, at best. And, they completely missed the point of who and what I truly am. Yet, they presented these False-Truths as the truth, and people believed them. I guess??? Has this ever happened to you?

This is just something to think about. You really should consider this whenever you hear anything that you hear; be it newsworthy, or otherwise. Ask yourself, who is saying what and why? Where have the obtained their facts? And, are they presenting a Full Truth or just the truth as they wish it to be perceived?

* * *

02/Aug/2025 02:05 PM

There's always tomorrow, until there isn't.

* * *
01/Aug/2025 12:07 PM

The only reason you ever get mad at someone is because they do something that you don't like.

Do you ever ask yourself the question, *"What gives me the right to cast my expectations onto anyone?"*

* * *
01/Aug/2025 12:06 PM

Just because you don't question the truth does not mean that the truth is not questionable.

TANGERINE DREAM
01/Aug/2025 07:58 AM

    I have seen that some people have defined me as an electronic musician. I guess that's true. …Defined by some definitions. I never really saw it like that, however. I feel like, music is music, and however you create it, you create it. Who needs the definitions?

    I remember when I was maybe twelve, or just into my teens, I lived in this dumpy furnished one-bedroom apartment with my mother over on 6th Street, in the area of L.A. that later became known as Koreatown. It was the summer. And, as is common with young people on their summer break, there was a lot of lost time.

    I remember this one moment when I began creating this rhythm on the metal shelfing section of our coffee table. I guess it was set up to keep magazines in or something. I created this rhythm by banging it with my hands. I could just feel the rhythm and the sound and the essence. I knew if there was only some way to record that sound, I would really have something. Of course, that was long before the world where we find ourselves today. Back where recording anything, with any quality, was very expensive. So, it was all lost. But I knew… There I was, just a coffee table and me… It could have been a great something had it been captured.

    If you ever think about it, really, all music is pretty much the same. Whatever era you find yourself within, there is a constant, a standard, a definition that defines the music. …An expected something that you expected to hear.

    Most people don't think about this, however. But, who's fault is that?

    Anyway… As my music moved farther away from the traditionally expected, yes, the instruments that make up the realm of electronic music have become part and parcel of my craft.

But, let's step back a little bit. Ever since I first heard, and was thankful flush enough to possess the resources to purchase the first widely embraced 1974 album by the band Tangerine Dream, *Pheadra,* I have been inspired by their creation. Back then, it truly shook me. It was Satori. It was a revelation. I would put my headphones on and just become emersed into its essence.

To this day, that album still holds strong!

A few years later, in 1977, the William Freidkin film, *Sorcerer,* was released. Tangerine Dream provided the soundtrack for that film. Again, it was inspiriting.

As I watched that film in the movie theatre, over in Westwood, with my friend, I felt like I possessed a knowledge that no one else knew, based on my understanding of the band. The masses were only introduced to their music via the film. Me, by that point, I knew all about them. Knew, before knowledge was so easy to come by.

Every now and then, when I'm creating music, especially electronic music, there will be a moment when I feel that impact of Tangerine Dream. As I commonly use vintage synthesizers, sometimes I will touch a sound that they previously invoked. That happened to me today.

Now, let's keep in mind... Tangerine Dream is, without a doubt, one of the, if not the, most influential electronic bands of all time. If you don't believe me, just watch the film Sorcerer. Listen to its soundtrack. Then, keep your ears open when you hear the soundtrack of many of the films of today. What do you hear? Answer: A sound that they pioneered.

Now, I am not, (necessarily), talking about what the band became, with its oh-so-many, ever-changing, members. But, Edgar Willmar Froese, its founding member, revolutionized everything.

When I hit those notes today, it reminded me of a moment in my life. It must have been 1988 or 1989. I was invited to a costume party on Halloween. This was the only costume I ever accepted the invitation to.

I was invited by this beautiful architect woman, who was ALL into me, at the time. I know, I know… I should have paid her more mind, as she was a great-great human being, and an excellent catch. But, back then, my mind was all over the place and I had so many women on the line. I was deeply in the game and I just did not succumb to her many advances. My mistake!

Anyway, I remember she told me this party was hosted by one of the members of Tangerine Dream. She told me this, I guess, to suck me into coming.

I guess, I should have been impressed. But, I don't even know which member of Tangerine Dream he was??? Again, there was and are, so many.

I've never been a fame whore or a star struck individual. I grew up in L.A. and famous people were all around me my whole life. No biggy. But, for whatever reason, I decided to show up. My bro, Vinchenzo in tow.

I know she introduced me to the guy. But, the party was blank, like so many parties are. I hate parties! Though I have memories of the event. I don't remember the guy at all. This is about all I can say of the saying.

Vinchenzo and I had a few drinks, talked to a few sweet young ladies, and bailed. There was this great goth club going on back then, over on Sunset near Western, our home turf, and we both way wanted to be there more than at the party. I mean, hey, it was Halloween. Plus, they loved us at that club. We were the O.G.s

But, before I get too far off point…. Which I think I already have…

Does it matter how you create what you create as long as you created it? For years my focus of music creation was the guitar. Keyboards came later. But, when they did, what I found was the pathway to the essence of the abstract.

Which, as you may have guessed, is more where my mind finds its solace.

So, one can throw definitions all that they want. One can try to find a means to categorize the all and the everything, if they choose to. But, no matter what definition you put on something, if there is no definition intended, does that definition mean anything at all?

Most people need to possess structure in their life. That allows them to find some sort of semblance. But, the true meaning of life and things and people and all of that is an illusion. How many times have you thought some thing or some one was one way, only to find out later that you were totally wrong? So, who was wrong? You for casting the definition? Or, that other entity for being what they truly were, definition-less?

You can try to categorize things. You can attempt to hold everything and everyone to some sort of a mold. But, that mold is only defined by your own mind. Your mind is not their mind. Your mind is not my mind. Thus, how does your definition of anything or anyone hold any true validity?

Understand this, and you are free.

THE SON OF THE BUDDHA
31/Jul/2025 02:26 PM

Siddhartha Gautama, known as, *"The Buddha,"* has long commanded scholarly attention for his journey to enlightenment and the profound doctrines he imparted. In contrast, considerably less focus has been devoted to his only child, Rāhula. Nevertheless, Rāhula's life presents valuable insight into the interplay of personal legacy, familial obligation, and the renunciation intrinsic to Buddhist philosophy.

Birth and Early Life

Rāhula, whose name translates to *"Fetter,"* or, *"Bond,"* was born in the royal palace of Kapilavastu to Prince Siddhartha and Princess Yasodhara. His birth is recognized within Buddhist tradition as a pivotal moment, coinciding with Siddhartha's decision to renounce his royal heritage in pursuit of spiritual awakening. The arrival of a son embodied both emotional joy and a symbolic connection to worldly responsibilities, reinforcing the very attachments the Buddha would ultimately leave behind.

Raised amidst the Shakya kingdom's affluence by his mother and extended family, Rāhula's early years unfolded in the absence of his father, who had embarked on his quest for enlightenment—a journey that would shape religious history.

Buddha's Return

Upon attaining enlightenment, the Buddha returned to Kapilavastu to disseminate his teachings among family and subjects. This significant reunion brought him face-to-face with his wife, Yasodhara, and his son, Rāhula. According to canonical texts, Yasodhara encouraged Rāhula to seek out his father and request his inheritance. In response, Rāhula approached the Buddha, who discerned that true inheritance lay not in material wealth but in spiritual guidance. Consequently, he instructed the disciple Sariputta to ordain Rāhula as a novice monk (sāmaṇera), marking a watershed in the tradition.

Rāhula's Ordination and Monastic Life

Rāhula became the inaugural sāmaṇera in the Buddhist sangha, thereby establishing a precedent for ordaining children. Yasodhara's consent underscored her deep faith and willingness to uphold the Dharma, despite the sorrow expressed by family members such as King Suddhodana. The event underscored the transformative influence of the Buddha's teachings.

As a novice, Rāhula received guidance from the Buddha and leading disciples, including Sariputta and Moggallāna. He distinguished himself through humility, discipline, and an eagerness to learn. The Buddha frequently cited Rāhula as an exemplar in sermons emphasizing honesty, self-discipline, and mindfulness—virtues foundational to monastic life. *"The "Rāhula Sutta,"* for instance, records the Buddha's counsel to his son regarding introspection and ethical behavior.

The Teaching of Rāhula

The discourses delivered to Rāhula represent cornerstone texts in Buddhist ethics. The Buddha advocated rigorous truthfulness, self-reflection, and the exercise of restraint and compassion. Notably, in the, *"Ambalatthika Rāhulovāda Sutta,"* he advised Rāhula to assess the consequences of any action before undertaking it, a guideline integral to Buddhist practice.

Attaining Enlightenment

Over time, Rāhula advanced steadily in the monastic discipline, strictly adhering to precepts and deepening his understanding of the Dharma. Tradition holds that Rāhula ultimately achieved Arhatship, attaining liberation from the cycle of rebirth, *"Saṃsāra,"* at the age of eighteen. Both Theravāda and Mahāyāna traditions celebrate this accomplishment, venerating Rāhula as a model of youthful dedication and spiritual attainment.

Rāhula in Buddhist Literature and Iconography

Rāhula occupies a nuanced position in Buddhist literature, depicted as an earnest and obedient figure in scriptures. His story is referenced in Jataka tales and other commentaries to underscore themes of obedience, discipline, and the universality of spiritual potential.

In Buddhist iconography, Rāhula commonly appears as a young monk alongside the Buddha and prominent disciples. His example continues to inspire novice practitioners, reinforcing ideals of virtue and perseverance in monastic settings worldwide.

While a significant figure in Buddhism and a symbol of the potential for spiritual growth, Rāhula is said to have died at a young age, before the Buddha and some of his other prominent disciples.

Legacy and Significance

Rāhula's biography encapsulates fundamental Buddhist themes: the tension between attachment and liberation, the significance of renunciation, and the accessibility of enlightenment across social boundaries. His narrative not only exemplifies the expansive reach of the Buddha's teachings but also highlights the sacrifices made by those within the Buddha's immediate circle. For many adherents, Rāhula epitomizes the transformation of filial piety into spiritual aspiration. His journey demonstrates that the transmission of wisdom and the alleviation of suffering constitute the greatest inheritances a parent can bestow.

Rāhula's transition from prince to devoted monk, culminating in enlightenment, illustrates the profound efficacy of the Dharma. His life serves as enduring testimony to the possibilities inherent in renunciation and spiritual inquiry. Today, Rāhula is honored as an emblem of youthful virtue and the transcendent nature of the bonds between parent and child, as realized in the collective pursuit of truth and liberation.

In summary, Rāhula, the son of the Buddha, emerged as a dedicated monastic, attained enlightenment, and remains a venerated figure whose legacy conveys enduring lessons in humility, discipline, and spiritual awakening.

* * *
31/Jul/2025 11:55 AM

You don't know there's a problem until you know there is a problem.

THE WORLD IS A VISUAL THING
28/Jul/2025 01:37 PM

I don't know about what pops into your feed, on the various social media platforms, but I get at least a certain amount of young, very pretty girls, discussing all the things that young pretty girls discuss. And, they each seem to have grown a large following. I believe the reason why, in the all of this, is all pretty obvious. They are young pretty girls, and they send that desire of the possibility of hope into the minds of all the young (and old) men out there.

I guess the first wave of this happened with MySpace. The first true, highly embraced, social media platform. I know I've spoken about this in the past, but it was a great platform. Rarely a night would go by that I was wasn't asked to attend some band's performance and I was put on their guest list. Celebrity/friends would invite me to meet them at the Rainbow or the Troubadour or the Viper Room or the… via MySpace. It was great!!! And remember, I was in my forties by that point in history.

There were girls making it big back then, as well. Some were actually my friends. They would have a ton of people all about them, like many of the Influencers have today.

The thing is, that whole MySpace era, was like two decades ago. Sure, MySpace is still a thing, but they killed what it once was. Why, I guess I will never understand???

The thing is, and I guess the point to all of this, with time, people age. And, now when I look to some of those one-time famous MySpace people, time has gone past/their time has gone past. The once young women have become older. Many have grayed. Some have put on the pounds. All have aged. Like the great lyric from the Aerosmith song states, *"Every time that I look in the mirror. All these lines on my face getting clearer. The past is gone."* Some have even passed away.

I doubt that the whole Influencer Culture, of the back then, made the kind of money as they women seem to do now. But me, I always question, how are these people getting paid? And, who is paying them?

I think we would all love to make a grand living simply by doing a content bit like one that came into my feed today of this girl, eating at a restaurant, and then ranking the food she was eating. I mean really, who pays her for doing that?

I know as this whole Influencer Culture began to take hold, a lot of the girls would broadcast from their bedroom, with their bed behind them. I mean, come on… What a ploy. What a feed for the fantasy of the viewers. It always made me smile.

One the other side of this issue, at least just a little bit, there was this great television personality, Cheslie Kryst. Not only was she a beauty pageant winner but she had a degree in law and was on the bar of two separate states. Plus, she was a correspondent for the TV Entertainment News Show, *Extra*. She was gorgeous.

When the pandemic hit, and as we were all in isolation, she had to do some of her reporting from her apartment. There, she would broadcast from her bedroom. During one interview, the actor, Oma Epps, made some jokes about this fact and her bed being behind her. She stated, it was due to the WiFi reception being the best in her bedroom. Maybe that was true??? But, he read into it what most fantasy-seeking men would.

Sadly, soon after that, she took her own life. I think everyone asked the question, how could she do that? She had so much going on? But, she did.

Afterwords, her mother said she suffered from what is now termed, High-Functioning Depression. I've been suffering from that most of my life. Long before it had a title. So, though each case is somewhat different, I can understand what she was feeling. In my case, add in Chronic Anxiety

Disorder, most probably based upon a supremely fucked-up childhood, and, need I say it, I've been a mess most of my life. But, for her, it caused her to end her own life. Very Sad! She could have owned the world. For me, I can realize she was at the pinnacle of an ideal example of a person presented and exhibited to the world, which takes us back to the this of all that we are discussing here.

Like I say, of those who rose to the top of this game, way back in the way back when, there is a shelf-life. Then what? Where do they go from there/here?

I believe most people watch the content they watch and maybe enjoy what the person has to say or to present or to whatever... Certainly, there are some podcasters who aren't pretty young ladies, who shake the world with their platform. For them, then, they maybe can ride it out to a better degree, as they are not basing their appeal on their looks. But, as I have watched, some of those from that earlier era/some of those that I have personally known, are eventually left to the lost.

I believe we all need to think about this. Contemplate the what comes next. I mean, life changes, trends go away, platforms lose their favor, then what? If you don't have a plan for your next step in life, when everything becomes different, what are you going to do when it does?

YOU HAVE TO TAKE THINGS FOR WHAT THEY ARE WORTH
25/Jul/2025 04:23 PM

To tell the story... I was driving down the 22 last Sunday, coming home after visiting the antiques stores in Orange. This car jams past me, very-very fast; maybe like one hundred miles an hour. BAP a rock hits my front window, putting a large crack in it. I'm guess flung from the tires of that car. God damn it!

So, I put it off for a couple of days. Just not wanting to deal. But, then I make an appointment, and this AM I take my car to Safelite to have the windshield replaced.

They told me it would take about an hour when I made the appointment. So, I thought, okay, I'll just hang out. When I got there, however, they said it would be more like three hours. Fuck!

I didn't want to waste my day, so I called up an Uber. $45.95 to get me home. But, what could I do?

The driver was a nice guy; very talkative.

Really, I don't like to converse with Uber drivers or anybody. I'm really not a very friendly person anymore. Just too many times I've been fucked over by being nice. But...

We talked about him being an Uber driver since its inception. How he has had over fifty thousand rides. Wow! He spoke of how, in the early days, he used to make pretty good money. But now, they changed the pay scale and... He told stories of driving people from L.A. to Santa Barbara, to Fresno, and even to Vegas. That's crazy... I'm sure he has a lot of stories to tell with that much milage under his belt.

He got to speaking about how he used to live in a one-bedroom apartment with his wife and his three kids. The kids slept in the bedroom and his wife and him on a pullout couch in the living room. He spoke of how life was good then. Then, a two-bedroom opened up next-door. His wife wanted to move, so they did. From that, his rent went up nine hundred dollars. Now, they can't afford to go to Mexico to visit their family three times a year anymore.

It was a bit of a long drive from Safelite to where I live. So, a lot of talking went on. Nice guy.

I get home. I give the driver the top level, 5-Stars and a twenty-five percent tip. I do some work at home—go out and have lunch with my lady. Then, a few hours later, my car is ready. My lady drives me the forty minutes back to Safelite.

Driving home, I start to hear a lot of noise coming from my glass. That is not good or right. It continued to get worse. Damn it!

I called them. No answer. I texted them. No response. Finally, I get home and call the main number. A customer service rep puts me on hold, and calls the location where I had my work done, and I am set for a redo tomorrow. What a day/days life fucker. It's really annoying. I'm going to have to get up and take my car back to them early tomorrow morning. I'm definitely going to write another Yelp review about them. Last time I went there it was a four. This time it will be a one.

…Just a waste of time and money!

But, this is life, you know… This is the way it is. Some people don't give a fuck about the shitty jobs that they do. Most could care less about fucking over the life of someone else. They're getting paid, so who cares? It shouldn't be that way/I wish it wasn't that way. But, that is the way it is.

Truly, do you really care about the way you affect someone's life that you don't know? Do you really care if you cost them time and money and… If you do, good for you. You are one of the rare ones. If you don't, what does that say about you?

So, here we are. This is life. Sometimes, as the saying goes, *"Shit happens."* Then what? All you can really do is to take things for what they are worth and try to make the most of them. It's not right. It's not fun. But, what other choice do you have???

THE DISTRACTED MIND
25/Jul/2025 10:13 AM

How much of your Life Time do you allow your mind to simply wander—being driven from one thought to the next? If you commonly allow this to happen, do you ever contemplate what you are thinking about, why you are thinking it, and what benefit, or lack there of, those thoughts have on your life?

We are all driven by our emotions. That's just life. That's just human nature. But, what motivates the emotions that are radiating within your brain? For most, what they think about comes from outside stimuli. This outside stimulus comes from all sorts of sources. Maybe it is TV, radio, podcasts, internet content, the news, what someone is saying about someone or something else, or a million other things. The one place it does not come from is within you. You are driven by what you see and what you hear. So, what are you seeing and what are you hearing?

To some degree, what you see and what you hear is a choice. You chose the movies and the TV you watch, the content you view in your streams, what you listen to and whom you listen to. Yes, much of life is thrown at you, and you have no control over. But, beyond the all of that, you are the one who makes a choice to view and hear a good portion of what comes into your brain.

Most people never ask themselves the question of why? They simply do and are then driven by what they consume. How about you? How many questions do you ask of yourself about what you in-take?

After you have taken in that whatever it is you have consumed, do you ever question how that whatever affects your thought process, leading to your actions? How does it make you feel, equally what you do next?

I can say, all negative anything is only negative, and you should not let that into your life. But, look around you, how many people thrive on watching negative movies and listening to negative speak. How about you?

You see, this is the point where your mind is driven in a specific direction. Whether that be down a positive or a negative road. Thus, controlling your life.

Few people ever choose to take control over themselves and their in-take. They just accept the whatever and do nothing to control any of it. But, you can control it. You can, if you choose to. Do you choose to?

This is why so few people ever reach any higher state of consciousness. They just let life happen. They are controlled by whatever is feed into them, and they do what they do based upon little, if any, deep thought. How about you? How much control do you take over your thoughts?

Following is a previously published article I composed. It takes a deeper look into the mind of distraction. You may find it interesting.

The Distracted Mind in Buddhism
Understanding and Transforming Mental Restlessness Through Buddhist Teachings

Scott Shaw, Ph.D.

The phenomenon of the distracted mind is both ancient and universal. In Buddhist philosophy and practice, distraction—often referred to as, *"Monkey Mind,"* which is recognized as a fundamental aspect of human experience and a central challenge on the path to awakening. Buddhism offers time-tested insights and practical techniques to understand, manage, and ultimately transcend mental distraction, paving the way toward clarity, peace, and liberation.

The Nature of the Distracted Mind

At the heart of Buddhist thought lies the observation that the mind is inherently restless. In Pali, the term, *"Vicikicchā,"* often denotes doubt, indecision, and scatteredness, while, *"Uddhacca,"* refers more specifically to restlessness or mental agitation. The distracted mind jumps from one thought to another, much like a monkey swinging through trees—hence the common metaphor of the, *"Monkey mind."*

Distraction manifests as a continual flow of thoughts, memories, worries, desires, and sensory impressions that often pull attention away from the present moment. This mental restlessness is seen not as a personal failing, but as an intrinsic characteristic of an untrained or unenlightened mind.

Roots of Distraction

Buddhism teaches that the mind's tendency toward distraction is rooted in the Three Poisons: greed, *"Lobha,"* hatred, *"Dosa,"* and delusion, *"Moha."* These fundamental defilements give rise to craving, aversion, and ignorance, causing the mind to habitually seek pleasure, avoid discomfort, and become lost in confusion or fantasy. This cycle perpetuates distraction and prevents the deep, stable attention necessary for insight.

Distraction in the Context of Suffering

The Buddha identified suffering, *"Dukkha,"* as an inevitable part of existence and attributed much of this suffering to the mind's inability to remain focused and present. When attention is scattered, individuals are more likely to be swept away by emotions, react impulsively, or become entangled in rumination and worry.

The distracted mind feeds dissatisfaction by constantly seeking stimulation and novelty, rarely resting in contentment or peace. In this way, distraction becomes both a symptom and a cause of deeper existential disquiet.

Five Hindrances and Mental Distraction

In Buddhist teachings, the Five Hindrances, *"Pañca nīvaraṇāni,"* are seen as major obstacles to meditation and spiritual progress. Of these, two are particularly relevant to the distracted mind.

Sensory desire, *"Kāmacchanda:"* The craving for pleasant experiences pulls the mind outward, causing it to wander after sights, sounds, tastes, and other sensory objects.

Restlessness and worry, *"Uddhacca-kukkucca:"* Agitation, anxiety, and mental spinning prevent the mind from settling and focusing on the present moment.

The other hindrances—ill-will, sloth and torpor, and doubt—can also contribute to distraction, but sensory desire and restlessness are often most immediately felt during attempts to meditate or concentrate.

Buddhist Practices for Taming the Distracted Mind

Recognizing distraction is the first step in the process of transformation. Buddhist practice offers a variety of tools and teachings designed to cultivate concentration, *"Samatha,"* mindfulness, *"Sati,"* and wisdom, *"Paññā."*

Mindfulness

Mindfulness is the practice of bringing nonjudgmental, sustained attention to the present moment. In the Satipatthana Sutta, *"The Discourse on the Foundations of Mindfulness,"* the Buddha describes mindfulness of body, feelings, mind, and mental objects as a direct path to realization.

When distraction arises, mindfulness allows practitioners to notice the wandering of the mind, gently acknowledge it, and return attention to the chosen object—such as the breath or bodily sensations—without self-criticism.

Concentration Meditation

Samatha, or calm-abiding meditation, aims to develop deep states of concentration called, *"Jhānas."* By focusing on a single object, such as the breath, a candle flame, or a mantra, the practitioner gradually quiets the mental chatter and stabilizes attention.

Through repeated practice, the mind becomes more unified and less likely to be pulled by every passing thought or impulse. This steadiness creates the foundation for deeper insight.

Insight Meditation, "Vipassanā."

Vipassanā, or insight meditation, builds upon concentration and mindfulness. It involves observing the changing nature of thoughts, feelings, and sensations to gain direct understanding of impermanence, *"Anicca,"* unsatisfactoriness, *"Dukkha,"* and non-self, *"Anattā."*

By seeing that thoughts and distractions arise and pass away according to causes and conditions, practitioners become less identified with them and less prone to being swept away.

Loving-Kindness, "Mettā," and Compassion Practices

Cultivating positive mental states such as loving-kindness and compassion can help reduce anxiety and agitation, which are major sources of distraction. When the mind is suffused with goodwill, it is more likely to rest in contentment and less likely to seek escape in restless activity.

Ethical Conduct, "Sīla."

Buddhism emphasizes the importance of living ethically, as unwholesome actions tend to agitate the mind and fuel distraction. Practicing the Five Precepts—which include refraining from harming, stealing, sexual misconduct, false speech, and intoxication—creates the inner conditions for a peaceful and attentive mind.

Modern Perspectives:
Distraction in the Age of Technology

While the distracted mind has always been a challenge, the modern world—with its constant stream of digital information, notifications, and entertainment—has made distraction more pervasive and insidious than ever. Buddhist teachers have responded by emphasizing the timeless relevance of mindfulness and the urgent need to reclaim attention in the face of technological overload.

Applying Buddhist Understandings Today

Many contemporary practitioners find that integrating mindfulness into daily life is crucial. Simple practices such as conscious breathing, single-tasking, and taking periodic breaks from devices can help to anchor attention and create moments of presence amidst the busyness.

Monastic traditions often advocate periods of silence and retreat as a way to reset the mind and re-establish clarity. Even in everyday life, carving out moments for reflection, meditation, or mindful walking can foster resilience against distraction.

Transforming Distraction into Insight

Buddhism does not demonize distraction; rather, it treats it as a valuable teacher. Each moment of noticing distraction presents an opportunity to practice returning, again and again, to the present. Over time, this process builds patience, self-awareness, and equanimity.

Buddhism teaches that with sustained effort; the mind can be trained and transformed.

Through continuous practice, the distracted mind gradually gives way to deeper clarity, concentration, and, ultimately, liberation from suffering.

The distracted mind, though challenging, is not insurmountable. Through the lens of Buddhist philosophy, distraction is seen as a natural part of the human condition, one that can be observed, understood, and gently transformed through the cultivation of mindfulness, concentration, and ethical conduct. In learning to work skillfully with distraction, we discover a path not only to greater productivity or calm, but to profound freedom and the realization of our true nature.

THE HALL OF FAME
23/Jul/2025 01:22 PM

I'm sure I've written about this somewhere/sometime before, but the, (at least once-upon-a-time), numerous martial art hall of fames that were and are out there are quite a curious entity. Why, you ask? Because virtually all of them have its inductees pay to become inducted.

I don't know??? Is it just me??? But, I have always thought that was very strange.

The original martial art hall of fame, at least the first one that I knew about, was instigated by Black Belt Magazine. That one, at least initially, was developed around the best tournament fighters and kata performers, the best and most well-known instructors, the people who really made a contribution to the martial arts, and the like. Those awards were given out each year, no charge. That should be the way it should be, don't you think?

I had a strong working relationship with one of the original editors of that magazine, and even he said, it was all a very, *"Political,"* process, getting inducted. But, at least in my mind—at least back then, it was done the way it should be done, no charge to the inductees.

I always felt a bit jilted by not being inducted into the Black Belt Hall of Fame. I mean, I was, back when there were actually magazines being published and books being printed, one of the most prolific proponents of the Korean martial arts. Magazines and book publishers were contacting me all the time asking for content. But, I guess, I just wasn't on the inside of the inside. I don't know???

Things began to change with Black Belt, however. They started doing this thing where people could suggest who should be inducted into their hall of fame. I don't know how that really worked. I know a bunch of people nominated me, but??? I imagine that was only a suggestion box and the real choices all came from the top: i.e. the editor and/or the publisher. But, times all changed and all that went away.

Back in the back when, in the late stages of magazine publications and the early stages of the internet, there became tons and tons of martial art hall of fames. I mean, a lot. Those... I was asked to be inducted into a number of them. But, they all held a price tag. My answer always was the same, *"Thanks but no thanks."* I mean, what does a hall of fame actually mean if you have to pay to be inducted? Though, I know, a lot of people who did write that check.

I guess the point to all of this is, what do accomplishments actually mean? One would think, that if you actually do accomplish something good or great or grand or helpful or anything like that, that if someone likes it, they would simply compliment and award you for what you have done. Right? But, if you have to pay for that appreciation, doesn't that kill the whole process?

I mean, it's just like paying for rank advancement. Something that virtually every martial art school and martial art organization requires. I never did that. I never charged my students for rank advancement. If they were good enough, if they learned their stuff, that was all that matter to me. I never wanted to make money over something that they accomplished. But, that charging for rank is a universal trend. I've known so many people who would say and describe how they could not advance in rank because they could not afford the price of that advancement. My belief is, if they are deemed good enough, shouldn't that be the only price they have to pay to advance? I've never been in the military, but I have never heard of someone, in any branch of the service, paying to rise up in rank.

Now, I get it, the modern martial arts are all about business. I don't agree with that at all. I believe that mindset diminishes the true essence of these art forms. But, that is the way it is. I know I had to pay for all of my rank advancements, back when I was still seeking such things.

But, shouldn't advancement never be measured by how much money you have? This especially includes the various martial art hall of fames. If you are deemed good enough to be induced, shouldn't that induction be the gift of whatever organization is behind that award?

I do not believe that there are as many martial art hall of fames as there once was. So, here's a philosophic question for you, what does it mean if a person had to pay for being inducted into a martial art hall of fame that no longer exists? What hall of fame are they a member of?

This whole thought process is not limited to the martial arts. It really reaches out to all areas of life. Think how many people expect some sort of recompense for moving someone up the ladder. Do you? Do you make a person pay to get what you have to offer? If you do, what does that make you?

Most people hope to achieve something in their life. That's a natural thing. Most people are very happy when they are rewarded for what they have accomplished. But, doesn't it just diminish the all and the everything if they have to pay to get that award?

If you have to pay for it, is it an award at all?

OZZY IS GONE BUT NOT FORGOTTEN
22/Jul/2025 12:54 PM

It was on my mind, and I was going to write about an entirely different subject today but then, as I was driving home, it came over the news waves that Ozzy Osbourne died today at the age of seventy-six. That's sad.

Whether you loved or hated his music, there is no doubt that he was a Rock God. But, more than just that, his family and him helped to usher in a new genre of TV, Reality TV, with their show, *The Osbournes*.

There's a lot of things that can be said about Ozzy. His autobiography, I Am Ozzy, is a very revealing read. I suggest, if your feel like, that you check it out. It provides a lot of information.

I was a big fan of *Black Sabbath* during my teenage years in the 1970s. I saw them perform several times. Perhaps at the top of that list is when *The Ramones* opened for them at the Long Beach Arena. That was a great show. My mind had already shifted to Punk by that point in time, though the rest of the audience did not get it yet. But, what a combination, *The Ramones* and *Black Sabbath*.

When they kicked Ozzy out of the band, that was a hard pill to shallow. Though Ronnie James Dio gave it his best, that was just not *Black Sabbath*. Nor was it the real band with the long list of other singers they brought on board over the next decade or so.

I was never really a fan of Ozzy Osbourne as a solo artist. Though I certainly listened to and even liked a few of his song throughout the 1980s, as they were being played all the time from radio stations to MTV. But, my musical tastes had changed by then. I was more in remembrance of *Black Sabbath,* who I considered to the be the first truly Goth band.

All of the original members of *Black Sabbath* did reunite, truly for the last time, as it was billed, just a few days ago. Sadly, Ozzy was confined to a gothic wheelchair. But, he was still kicking it.

They haven't yet released the cause of Ozzy's death. I'm sure that will be coming in the near future. Kind of like Bukowski, with the lifestyle that Ozzy lived, it's kind of a surprise that he made it this far. But, he did. And, that was a great thing, as he never stopped making music.

You know, every now and then, we lose one of those cultural icons. And, love or hate them, you cannot deny their contribution. This was and is certainly the case with Ozzy Osbourne. RIP Ozzy.

* * *

22/Jul/2025 09:12 AM

Why do you want to be a follower?

YOU PEOPLE ARE SPEAKING ABOUT IT LIKE IT WAS YESTERDAY
21/Jul/2025 07:10 AM

  Do you ever watch really good cinema presentations like, *Noir Alley,* on TCM? Of course, as is well known for all of you who know anything about me, Cinema Noir is one of my favorite genera of cinema. But, that's not the point of the point to any of this. If you ever listen to Eddie Muller, or really any of the talking heads on TCM discussing the cinema of times gone past, they speak of it as if it were yesterday. Why, you ask? Because they did not live it. And, as such, as it is new to their minds, they speak on the subject as if it is all-new. But, it is not all-new at all. It was shot a million years ago. In fact, most, if not all, of the people associated with that film project, whichever film project they are discussing, are long gone.

  In many ways, this is the same with my Zen Cinema. People discuss and review it as if it were created yesterday. But, it was not. Much/most of what they discuss was created decades ago. Yet, they continue to talk.

  I guess that's a good thing; right? To have created something so long ago, yet people still discuss it to this day. I don't know??? What I do know is, they discuss it from the point of view of someone who did not live it. They can describe it, they can critique it, but they can never truly understand it, as they were not there; they did not live it.

  The reason I say all of this is that, look around you, look to your own mind, re-listen to your conversations, how much of what you think about and say about and decided about have you, personally, had no true involvement with? Yes, you may like a something or a person or a whatever. Yes, you may hate a something or a person or a whatever. But, none of that is you. That is just what you think, leading to what you say, maybe leading even to what you do, based upon something that has no true meaning or value to your life. Really, ask yourself, how much of what you think, or speak, leading to what you do, have you had nothing, personally, to do with?

If that is the definition of your life, then what is the definition of your life? Is your life, yours? Or, is it someone else's?

The people that look outside of themselves are the one who do not wish to face the what truly is within. They want to deflect people from looking and judging their life. Or, they simply have not created enough interesting elements to make their life a whole and complete entity onto itself.

This is why sport's team worship is so prevalent in modern society. This is why people worship musical groups. This is why people dive deep into the movies created by others. This is why people go to church. All of that and more gives their life something to think about. But, what are they doing, what are they creating, what are they truly living when all they think about is what someone else did or created?

* * *
20/Jul/2025 10:58 PM

If you believe that you have you something special to give to the world, that mostly likely means that you do not.

If you think you have something to teach, that mostly likely means that you do not.

If you deem that you know something special that someone else does not know, that mostly likely means that you do not.

* * *
20/Jul/2025 10:57 PM

How perfect is your life right now? If it is good, great! If it is not, ask yourself, *"What did you do to the life of that someone else, to make their life less than perfect?"* When you answer that question to yourself with truth, you will understand your condition.

HOW MUCH IS YOUR LIFE WORTH?
20/Jul/2025 07:06 AM

How much is your life worth? I'll let you know the answer to that question in a moment.

I was in this large antique store yesterday, and something caught my eye.

For those of us of a certain age, you will remember that if you went to public school, (I don't know about private school), each year they would take a photograph of the students. Those photos were oftentimes not very good but… In any case, near the end of the school year, they would offer to sell you a set, in varying sizes, of that photograph. If you bought it, you would also get an 8X10 sheet of small photos presenting all of your classmates. Remember???

Anyway, as I was walking through the store, this photo album caught my eye. It was opened to a page that presented one of those class photos. Looking at it, it was dated to the early 1950.

I picked up the photo album and checked it out. In association with class pictures over a number of years, it also presented all of these childhood photographs of this one young blonde girl growing up. It also had a few awards of merit and things like that from her school years. This caused me to wonder what had happened to this once young girl. I goggled her, and as she had a rather unique family name, her obituary photo immediately popped up. There she was, the onetime young blonde girl, now/then very old in the photo. Gone. Passed away.

Someone had obviously simply discarded this young girl, turned adult, childhood photo album. Probably to this woman, and maybe to her immediately family, those photos truly meant something—a reminder of a life lived. But then, whomever took ultimate possession of that album didn't care about the memory or the memories of that woman and tossed it to the wind, ending up in an antiques store. I thought to buy, to hold onto to that woman's life just a little bit longer. To give her/the world that one last glance at the memories of a person's life that was once alive. But, I decided to leave that to someone else.

Even more than this, think about your own life. Think of all of the memories you have. Think of all of the people you've met, the experiences you've had, the feelings, the emotions, the loves, the hates, the all, and the everything. Just like this woman, you too… Someday you will be gone, and no one will cared about what you care about. Really, think about it…

So, how much is your life worth? Let me answer that question for you, $15.00. That was the price tag on the photo album.

THE CHAIR HAS BEEN RENTED
17/Jul/2025 09:05 AM

Kinda funny… I noticed this picture of a Hindu god come up in my feed. It came from the account of one of those people who posts a lot of that stuff, all in the proclamation of being spiritual. It had a few sentences in Sanskrit below the image. In reading it, it looked kind of off, however. So, I decided to pop it over to google translate. Here's what it actually, said, *"The real courageous decorator owner. The game will be played for sure, the chair has been rented."* Of course, this made me smile.

I remember back in the days when there were all these people selling promised martial art rank and rank certificates out of magazines like Black Belt. FYI: That's where and how a lot of the old-schoolers got the high rank they possess, via pseudo-businesses like that. But, anyway… Every now and then, it would be brought to the attention of the greater whole how the words on those certificates, oftentimes in some Asian language, were totally wrong. They got them from somewhere, put them on the certificates, and who would know the difference, unless you knew the difference? I remember one time it was revealed the Chinese characters on this one company's certificate were actually taken from a Chinese restaurant menu. Pretty funny…

I guess all of this comes down to knowing what you know and/or believing what you believe. I know, in my lifetime, I have witnessed some people going to all length to back a lie they were told, or the lair who told it. They did this will all vigor. But, that did not change the truth of the lie. Then what?

I suppose what do words really mean anyway? Have you ever been in a situation where you are surrounded by people speaking a language you do not understand? They know what they're talking about. But, you do not. How does that change your experience?

Yet, think about it, all of these people from the West who have turned to Asian culture for art, inspiration, the martial arts, or religion, but they don't speak the language. Are the truly understanding anything?

Maybe they are, maybe they aren't? Yet, it goes on all around us, all the time. People believing something presented from a language, a culture, or a time in history they do not truly understand.

From a much more Zen perspective, what do words mean anyway? If you take out the context. If you don't care that the person who posted that posting was trying to appear to be all knowing and all spiritual, in someways, don't the words that he (or she) posted provide a pathway to some deeper truth, just like a koan? *"The real courageous decorator owner. The game will be played for sure, the chair has been rented."* Think about it.

* * *

16/Jul/2025 10:44 PM

If you're looking for someone to blame for something that has gone wrong in your life, the person to blame is generally yourself.

RECYCLED
16/Jul/2025 02:36 PM

I've been a photographer for most of my life. I got my own, (personal), camera when I was eight. A Kodak Instamatic. Loved that camera. Though, in looking back, those cameras, as popular as they were, took horrible photographs. The lens was just plastic crap. So, the image quality was terrible.

I got my first 35mm camera when I was in junior high; 7th grade. I had this rather forward-thinking instructor who actually offered a photo class to his young students. There, we learn to compose shots, and to develop film, and all of that good stuff. I really liked that class.

At Hollywood High School, I did an independent study photo class. Again, offered by a foreword-thinking instructor, where all I was asked to do was to take photographs and be as creative as possible. Then, one-on-one with the teacher, we would discuss each shot.

I collected all of those photographs in a manila folder decades ago. When I look back on them, they always make me smile. My-my how times and creative visions change…

Over the years, I advanced with my photo techniques and my camera equipment. Back in the 80s I used to carry three camera bodies and multiple lenses, in an over the shoulder bag with me, all across the globe. Man, that was heavy. What was I thinking?

My lady, she is a real pro photographer. She has the BFA to prove it. But, we always go back and forth, as I feel she doesn't compose her shots very well. *"Here let me show you how you should have composed the shot,"* I'm always jokingly telling her. And headshots, forget about it. She just doesn't get it. *"I'm a creative photographer, not a portrait photographer,"* she always exclaims. Though I have roped her into photographing all of my books on the martial arts.

Throughout all of this time, as time went along, there was a time, when I had a shit-ton of cameras and lenses and filters and flashes and light meters and all of that kind of nonsense. This was amplified when I got into the film game. But, I'm not a hoarder. And, if I'm not using something, and if it doesn't have a sentimental meaning to me, eventually I move all unnecessary stuff along. The thing is, when you live like that, more times than not, I am left wishing I had kept something as I often have to end up repurchasing it.

A new lens for my DSLR camera arrived today. Popped it on. Loved it. The thing is, as anyone in the photo or film game knows, you really need to keep your lenses protected, as that is the sourcepoint for capturing your images. Thus, you always need a UV filter for it.

Again, once upon a time, back in the long ago and the far-far away, I literally had hundreds of various lens filters, UV and otherwise, in all kinds of sizes. Years back now, with all of the vast advancements in photo enhancements in the digital realms, I thought I will never use any of these filters ever again. So, goodbye. I'm sure someone at the Salvation Army or the Goodwill loved it when they discovered that batch. But, they were probably just a reseller and put them up for sale on eBay. But, anyway…

I asked my lady did she have, *"Any UV filters left hiding anywhere?" "No."* So, I had to go to Amazon and order one up. It'll be here tomorrow.

I think this is always the dilemma in life. If you are a creative, you need whatever you need to bring those creations to life. But, unless you live in some big sprawling mansion, with an untold number of rooms, there is only so many places you can store your creative stuff. Thus, if you are like me, periodically, you let the unused go. But, then what? Then what, if you need it, a bit farther down the line?

Weird dilemma, I get it. But, if you know what I'm talking about, you know what I'm talking about.

So, you can keep something forever and never use it. Or, you can put it out there into the ethos, and let someone who will actually use it, put it to use.

    Collecting, hoarding, or setting all things free, when they need to be set free… Which do you believe is the best thing to do? But remember, either way you choose it, there will always be a price to pay. Which price do you want to pay? The price of hoarding or the price for setting things free and then having to repurchase them?

WE COULD HAVE BEEN FRIENDS
15/Jul/2025 01:16 PM

    I always find it interesting how when you meet someone, sometimes you hit it off immediately. Other times, it takes some time to get to know a person and then you become friends. In other cases, you meet someone, and though you may both have common interests, because of what they did, said, or how they behaved, you immediately reject them from getting any closer to you. Yet, under different circumstances, you come to understand that had things been different, had they behaved differently, they may have become your friend.

    I saw an interesting little tidbit in my feed the other day. It was this guy discussing how when you are young, friendships are so much easier to create. You meet, you have a common interest, and you start hanging out. When you are an adult, however, you only allow new people into your life that have something to offer you. You don't have the time to waste doing naught with people that bring nothing to your life.

    I know I have felt that way for a long time. People try to come into my life, but as they provide no benefit for me hanging out with them, it's not that I reject them, I simply do not put in the time or the effort to spend time with them.

    From a person perspective, it seems that, particularly since I entered the film game some thirty plus years ago, that the only people that want to cozy up to me are those who want something from me or want me to do something for them. This has, of course, evolved over the years; the what I could do for that certain individual. Yet, it has remained a constant. There never seems to be anyone coming up and offering to do something for me while extending a hand of friendship. All of this has made me very standoffish.

    But, I get it… That's life. People want to move up and to achieve and to become, and all of that kind of stuff.

Like the guy who spoke in that reel said, *"As an adult, you only allow new people into your life that have something to offer you."*

I think we've all let people into our life that later we realized that doing so was a mistake. There's a million reasons for this, all due to that other person's actions or behavior. But, there we are, left with the what we are left with after they did whatever they did to us that messed up our life.

In life, why have you become friends with anyone you have ever become friends with? Did you ever ask yourself this question during the formative stages of your growing friendship?

In life, why have some of your friends fallen away? Was it something they did? Or, did they leave you behind because of something you did? And, what did that loss of friendship mean to both your life and their life?

I believe that one of the ultimate elemental truths in life is, people generally only do something that benefits them, whether knowingly or not. Friendship is no different. Though you may not want to admit this fact to yourself, ask yourself this question, did you ever maintain a friendship with anyone who brought nothing positive to your life?

Friendship is a complicated thing. There is all of these things in terms of personality, lifestyle, desires, and a million other elements that come into play in friendships. If you do not take the time to know your reason why for either pursuing or being in a friendship, then you really have not taken the time to know yourself. Think about all of this…

INTERVIEW:
THE ROLLER BLADE SEVEN DOCUMENTARY
15/Jul/2025 07:10 AM

I was kicking around here in the late-late night, as I tend to do. Another bottle of the grape gone down. I was sitting back watching what YouTube dished my way on the 85 inch and, out of the blue, came up, *Interview: The Roller Blade Seven Documentary.*

Though certainly, I was the one who lived what took place in that doc and I was the one who created the film itself, I hadn't watch it for a long-long while. As it was there/as YouTube had dished it my way, I took it as a sign and thought, *"What the hell,"* I gave it a watch. Damn, that's a good doc. It really captures the moment of what Don and I created and lived in that space in time.

It's always kind of funny to me, the people who talk and talk, write and write, and do whatever it is they do in relation to the negative about The Roller Bade Seven and other films—not just mine but everyone's. All I have to say is, *"Fuck you! What have you created?"* And, *"They're the ones talking about me, I'm not the one talking about them."*

RB7 and the path of cinema that was created in the process of that film's creation, and what came after, was and is revolutionary. But, I get it, if you weren't there, and you didn't live it, you, most probably, can never truly understand it.

I guess it's like all art. The art is for the artist. Everyone else, all they can do is critique it, talk about it, discuss it, review it, maybe think about it, but they can never truly live it. And, like I suppose I've said a million times before, the artist creates art, what does everyone else do? Discuss the art someone else has created.

So, if you feel like it, and if you get a chance, take a watch of that film, the first Zen Documentary. If you have already seen it—if it isn't your first go-round, even you may find some new understanding about, *Zen Filmmaking,* Donald G. Jackson, and myself. Or, you may not??? In either or any case, it may provide you with some insight into the creation of the first two Zen Films and to the mind of yours truly, Scott Shaw, (at least at that moment of history).

WHEN YOU'VE DONE NOTHING WRONG
14/Jul/2025 01:13 PM

Don't you hate it when you've done nothing wrong but the person who has done something wrong blames you or gets mad at you for what they have done?

I'm sure we've all gone through situations like that. I know I have. And, though I have tried and tried to understand what was the motivation of that other individual, I come up blank. They are just doing what they are doing based upon something that is lodged only in their own mind.

I had one of those situations occur to me today. I was driving along, and I come up behind a rather junky blue BMW and the driver is basically totally stopped at a stop sign. I'm guess his eyes were locked on his phone, doing whatever it was he was doing, and he didn't realize or care that there are other people in the world. I give it a few seconds, and then give a friendly honk of my horn. Instead of doing what most of us would do, as we all have been in that situation, and give a little wave of, *"Sorry,"* and drive on, the guy finally starts to drive off, but he does so at like zero miles an hour, just to instigate the situation farther. Please… As I grab the other lane and drive past his very slow-going car, he looks out his open window and give me one of those hard stares, like it was me who had done something wrong. Of. Course, this makes me laugh. And, like I always say, *"You better know who you're dealing with before you break hard on them."*

Anyway, had it been any normal situation, he would have driven on, and I would have driven on. The situation would have totally been forgotten in a moment or two. But, due to his behavior, here it is, locked in this blog forever.

It's kind of like I had to go to a funeral this past weekend. It used to be that I had a rule, *"No weddings and no funerals."* Why? Weddings are such a waste. People spend all of that time, all of that energy, and all of that money creating these big affairs. Then, a few years deep, they get divorced, they hate each other, and one or the other of them gets totally fucked over financially and has to turn over the house, the car, and pay them alimony or palimony forever. Man, the karma in all of that!

Funerals, I just do not like to celebrate death, as it is always not in a positive way, but always dug so deep in sorrow and remorse.

That used to be my rule, but then you get dug in deep with a partner who has a big family, who you know, and there is no way out. No excuse that can be made. You are expected to be there.

Anyway... It was kind of like the eulogy at this funeral... The daughter was crying as she spoke, questioning why her father had to suffer so much when he was such a good parent. The man died of lung cancer which had apparently metastasized to his mouth and gums and stuff. And, I understand, that is a hard, fucked up way to die. I guess he went through a lot of chemo and stuff. But, he was a smoker. Didn't he bring all that on himself?

I mean, yes, we can feel sympathy for the man and his family. But, wasn't it him who chose to create the situation that caused him to suffer and then to die?

And, I guess this brings us to the root in all of this, what fault is yours in whom you blame? What did you do to cause it? Or, what didn't you do to cause it?

Few people are honest with themselves. Few people are real with themselves. They want to blame all of the out there. But, when you are the one to blame, who else is to blame? If what is occurring is based upon what you did, who can you blame but you?

So, think about this the next time you are casting blame, especially when it is blame that you are casting for something that you created. Think about this the next time someone blames you for what they did. Because no matter how much someone wants to shift the blame, there is always one person who is truly at fault.

    Be real with yourself, when you are at fault. And mostly, don't let others drag you into their melodrama when they are the one who did that something wrong. Don't let them blame you when you are not the one to blame.

THE CALL TO MEDITATION
12/Jul/2025 07:42 AM

Throughout the centuries of human existence, the benefits of meditation have been proclaimed as one of the most essential tools for human development. Not only as a means to calm the racing mind and bring down the blood pressure, but, for those with a true passion for the absolute, as a method to reach enlightenment. Though this has been the understood proclamation, how many people truly meditate? Do you?

In the Hindu tradition, for example, it is taught that one should be awoken at Brahmamurta, which is about 4:00AM, each day. Then, get up, perhaps wash your face, and go and sit. Maybe you do some calming pranayama exercises and then fade into meditation. I know when I was in India, at the ashram, that is what we did.

I always found meditation a bit hard to accomplish when it is performed in this manner, however. I mean, one, you are awoken so early in the morning. Two, as it is so early in the morning, your mind has the tendency to want to go back to sleep. I was pretty good at staying awake. But, I would notice people sleeping all around me in the meditation hall.

Even before that point in my life, as a young, teenage zealot, I used to set my alarm for 4:30 AM to be awoken and go into meditation. Though, this didn't last too long, as, again, it was very early, and when you are alone, and the only one meditating, it can of cause your mind to question what you are doing and why.

In the more modern forms of mediation, commonly at the end of a class on hatha yoga, or even at the end of class at the martial art studio, students are guided to sit down, close their eyes, and meditate. Though this, of course, is a good and understood practice, and the timing for it seems ideal. But, at the end of any class so much is obviously going through your mind, especially after something like a martial art class, true meditation is hard to achieve; especially since it is only performed for such a short period of time.

Thus, we are left with a dilemma, when is the best time to meditate? Now, first all, as all of you who know me, or know of me, understand, I am a proponent of the fact that we must make all of life activities into a meditation. For that is where true satori may be found. This being said, if one does not develop the ability to consciously, and at will, turn off their thinking mind, then they will forever be guided by those racing thoughts which can lead to not only bad decisions but to a life defined by the random chaos of emotion and desire.

To truly learn how to meditate, one must first master the concept of turning off the mind. I know from the dawn of time many people complain that, at best, they can only do this for a few seconds. But, that is where practice and meditative training comes into play. The reason most people do not possess the ability to truly meditate is because they do not train their mind in the methods of meditation. Maybe they do it for a moment or two here or there. Maybe they try it at the end of that hatha yoga class. But, what they do not do is to make it a part of their lifestyle. If they do make it a part of their lifestyle, if they do, do it every day, then the understanding of how to actually meditate will find its way into your being. But, you have to try! And, you have to try for a long time.

So, this brings us back to the question of when is the best time to meditate? From my perspective, this is an individual choice. Sure, as has been proclaimed forever, meditation may best be accomplished if you do it at the same time, in the same quiet space, every day. But, as all of us who live in this modern world understand, that may not always be doable. Thus, you should not let that be the only defining factor. If you can do it every day, at the same time, in the same space, great. If not, that does not mean that you should meditate every day. Or, at least, at every chance you get.

The main thing you've got to do is to make meditation a part of your life. Every day, promise yourself you will sit and do it. You will take a few minutes, or longer, everyday; whether this be in the morning, midday, or at night before you go to bed, and turn off your mind.

The benefits of its practice have all already been discussed forever. So, I won't bother you with them here. What I will say is that, if you train your mind to be silent, you will have advanced your consciousness to a level that is known by only a few. You will have gained a vast new insight into our ability to hold your racing mind and your emotions at bay. Then, when you need to consciously silence your mind, you will possess the ability to do so.

WHAT YOU SEE IS WHAT YOU GET
11/Jul/2025 09:34 AM

Have you ever watched any of those, *"Real Housewives of..."* shows that are, (at least initially), broadcast here in the U.S. on the Bravo Network. They've been around for quite a while by this point in time, starting with *The Real Housewives of the O.C.,* then *Beverly Hills,* then...

If you watch them, what you will witness is how many of the cast members are so self-orientated, so self-serving, so selfish, so backstabbing that they go at life and they go at each other without a care for anyone but themselves. They do this until they are caught doing what they are doing. After they are caught, they lie, they deny, and they make excuses for their actions. It's really a scary microcosm of life.

In some cases, over time, you can see how fame has really taken hold of some of them, causing them to become this next worse version of themselves.

Most of the time, on these shows, what is portrayed is not filled with happiness or help-full-ness, but only conflict, arguing, backstabbing and self-serving behavior.

These are popular shows. Obviously, they are as the franchise has expanding to many cities, with many offshoots. My lady has watched a couple of these shows since their inception. I really dislike them, however. I hate to see people behaving in that manner. And, I really hate to be hit in the face with a world of self-serving conflict. My lady exclaims, *"That's real life."* But, is it? Maybe it is, but does it have to be?

I know there is conflict in this world all over the place. I understand that people only think about themselves, and most, generally, have very little care about others unless those others serve their decided upon greater purpose in some way. But...

It's kind of like two days ago, when I was driving down this street. This new BMW comes jamming past me and others, swerving in and out of cars, driving between lanes, and doing some really crazy shit to get where he was trying to go. I steered clear, of course. Up ahead, I see him coming up towards a large intersection. He jams around this rather junky SUV, via the median and into the left turn lane where the SUV was traveling and totally sideswipes the front fender of the SUV. The driver of the SUV stops, wondering, *"What the fuck,"* I would imagine. The driver of the BMW, now with the side of his nice new car scraped and smashed in, slows down for a second, and then jams off. He got aways with it. But, at what price? He didn't care. Maybe he's got a lot of money and fixing his car is no big deal. But, what about the driver of the SUV?

That's not too different from this other situation I witnessed about two months ago. It simply had a slightly different outcome. I was driving down the 110 freeway and this brand new red Ferrari comes jamming past at a hundred plus miles an hour. The driver was swerving in and out of traffic. I obviously took notice of the car and its speed, but I've witnessed that kind of nonsense before. A few miles up the road traffic starts to greatly slow. When I pull past, the driver of the Ferrari is standing out in the middle of the freeway next to his totally destroy car. You know, Ferraris are not built to take a hit. He obviously clipped another car, due to his speed and his not caring about any other driver, and BAM that was the end of that. The Ferrari was toast. There he stood, surveying the damage he had instigated.

The moral of these two tidbits… People only caring about themselves cause vast damage to not only the lives of other people, but to themselves.

Watching shows like, *The Real Housewives,* you (me) can't help but question, why would you associate with a person like that? I know, I know… The answer is money and fame. And sure, that's why the powers-that-be at that network cast people like that, people who will cause a controversy. That's what people, like my lady, like to watch, these dumpster fires in action. But, that does not have to be your world.

I know, in life, we are each going to encounter people who are not all that nice. I know I have. I know I've had to deal with some liars, some stealers, some judgers, some backstabber, some self-thinking hurters of other people. So yeah, *"That's real life,"* as my lady proclaims. But, I don't want to be a part of that. I don't want to be reminded of that. I don't want to take part in a life defined by that style of behavior. I certainly do not want to watch it on TV.

So, as is pretty much the case with at least most of the things that I write in this blog, it all comes down to you. What do you create? And, why do you create it? Do you create a world, dominated by what you want, defined by whatever it is you can do, be it good, bad, or otherwise to get it? Are you a fame, power, or money whore who is only trying to get what you can get, so you can flaunt it to the world and live that so-called, *"Perfect,"* life, however it is you define that to be? And, who and what have you hurt to get there? Who and what are you hurting right now? Who and what have you destroyed, like that Ferrari, on the freeway just so you could jam past everyone, pretending to be better and more than the everyone else? What have you caused to occur by you driving too fast just because you can?

Many people in this world are not good people. Many people in this world do not care about anyone else but themselves. Many people in this world lie to cover up their negative actions; both to others and themselves. But, if you get to where you get to, with pain and suffering in your wake, where have you actually gotten? What have you actually gotten? And, what will be the ultimate consequences of what you have done?

WORKING WITH OTHERS
10/Jul/2025 01:56 PM

For anyone who has ever made a film, you understand that it is a collaborative process. Each individual of the cast and the crew brings an element of something to the greater whole and the overall team. Yes, there must always be one captain of the ship. Someone who's keeps the focus and will preserve the overall direction of the project moving forward. But, it is each individual element that crates the overall vibe and destiny of the eventually finished film. And this goes to all areas of life. Not just filmmaking.

Now, this is not to say that all of the players on the team hold a positive mindset. There is always that someone who seems to throw the proverbial monkey wrench into the gears. What is their motivations? Who Knows??? But, if they do attempt to do that, it is the rest of the team that must come together to find a means to get that film finished.

…The stories I could tell you. And, have…

The reason I write this is that so often I receive questions about the films I have created in the earlier stages of my filmmaking career. People ask me about the cast, the crew, the equipment, the props, the techniques, and mostly about the process. All good! Happy to answer.

And certainly, there have been an untold number of reviews printed, filmed content created, and discussions among viewers of the early Zen Films. All good, as well. The only difference in the all of that is the fact that more often than not people get something wrong. And, from that wrong misinformation, fake news, is propagated. But, what can you (I) do?

The thing that I find interesting is that as *Zen Filmmaking* has evolved, few people have even taken notices of the evolution. I mean, once upon a time, *Zen Filmmaking* was on the lips of seemingly everyone. Back in the day, I have heard the term, *"Zen Filmmaking,"* voiced from the mouths of newscasters and anchors on entertainment TV shows—used as a means to describe when some A-listers decided to dive deep and employee avant-garde, improvisational filmmaking. The term's been used in magazine articles and books. But, is that all *Zen Filmmaking* is? Nothing more than a filmmaking style of cinematic creation based upon the fact that it does not employee screenplays? Not as far as I am concerned.

Again, the thing that I find interesting is that as *Zen Filmmaking* has evolved, few people have even taken notices of the evolution.

The last character-driven film I created was in 2009, *Vampire Abstract.* As I write this, that was sixteen years ago. Have I stopped making movies? Obviously not. I have made a plethora of them. But, they are not the ones that people discuss. They are not the ones that I am asked questions about. So, my question is, to the people that ask the questions and talk the talk about the Zen Films, *"Where have you been?"*

There was one guy, awhile back, who did a long-form view of one of my non-narrative Zen Films on YouTube. If you search for it, you may be able to find it. I think it's probably listed in my, *"Favorites,"* playlist on my YouTube channel. But, other than that, that's it.

Now, this may be a good thing. Maybe people are only watching them and allowing them to be as they are. Not judging. But, the viewer count is so much less on those Zen Films than the ones from my deep dark past.

I get it, people want storylines, as that is what they are used to. (As anti-story as my Zen Films tend to be). But, that's not the evolution of *Zen Filmmaking.* In fact, I think what I have been creating, in the more recent years, is a pure presentation of Zen on films. No story. Just substance.

Kind of like the character, Cyrus exclaimed in the great movie, *The Warriors, "Can you dig it?"*

So, what am I saying here? What I am saying is that *Zen Filmmaking* has evolved. It moved away from being a multi-individualized filmmaking process to one that is more pure and certainly more Zen in its application and its presentation. It is no longer attempting to create a, *"Thing,"* but is instead moving towards a meditative nothingness. If you've truly meditated, you will understand what I am discussing.

Like I am so often asked, *"Would you ever make another Roller Blade Seven."* Sure, I would. I'd be happy to form a team, create the crew, the cast and the characters. But, of all of the people that ask me that question, not one of them has ever suggested how that film could/would be financed. They just want the finished project. The something to critique. The something to love or to hate. The something to talk about.

So, until that individual steps up with a budget in hand, *Zen Filmmaking* will remain in the realms of the pure Zen. No cast. No crew. No story. Just me, a camera, and the cinematic art.

Next time you see, hear, or read someone discussing the Zen Film of a time gone past, tell them, *"Get with the program. It's a whole new ballgame now."*

YOU CAN ONLY UNDERSTAND
WHAT YOU CAN ONLY UNDERSTAND
10/Jul/2025 08:55 AM

If you've ever had a furry friend, you will understand how you think of them as human. Sure, you know they are a cat or a dog or a whatever. But, in your mind, you see them through the eyes of a human and relate to them the same way as you do to other people.

If you've ever had a furry friend, you will understand how they love you the best way that they can love you. They relay to you loving messages, or tell you what they want or need via the methods they have at hand, be they a cat, a dog, or a whatever. They probably know you are something different from them, but all they can do is be what they can be. And, from that, they interact with you via the mind that they possess.

Here's the thing about life, you can only understand what you can only understand. You can only be what you can be. The problem arises when people try to project what they understand onto others. The problem arises when someone believes what someone else is thinking or doing is wrong. But, how can that be? That person is operating from the space they are operating from. They are living their life via the way they know how to live, and think, and do. They are doing an endeavor from the space that they are based upon and that they understand. And, here's the catch, they are it, they understand it, but you, (or anyone else), is not that, you are not them, so, in all truth, you don't get it at all. You can never be what they are. You can never know what they know. You can never truly understand what they are living. You can try to interpret it. But, that's all that is, an interpretation. It is not who or what they are.

Think about this the next time you are thinking that someone else is wrong. Think about this the next you don't like what someone else is saying or doing. Think about this the next time you judge.

You can love your furry friend. You can provide for them the best life that is possible. But, no matter how much you project onto them that they are something other than what they are, that is not/that is never is what they are truly are.

Let all things be what all things are. Let them exist in their own perfection. With this, the world becomes a much better place.

WHAT COMES NEXT?
09/Jul/2025 07:50 AM

One of the biggest realizations that you will ever receive in your life is the understanding that if you did not do that something, that next event in your life would not have happened. This particularly comes into focus when you do something—maybe you even think what you are doing is right or good, but then it blows up in your face and all you are left with is the negative consequences.

This is the simple reality of life, what you choose to do will set up the next set of circumstances in your life. If what you do is good, then good should come from it. Just as if what you do is bad or hurtful, then what do you expect will happen next? But, of course, in life there are all of these variables. Variable that no one can predict. This is where it all gets complicated.

Take a moment right now and bring to mind one of those things that you did that caused a chain reaction that brought discomfort to your life. First of all, why did you do it? Did you do it to help? Did you do it to hurt? Did you do it for selfish or selfless reasons? Did you even think about the possible consequences of your actions before you took them?

The thing is, most people are not very honest with themselves as they pass through their life. They do what they do in a very self-serving manner. They do what they do hoping to get the result they hope for. Most, rarely contemplate any possible consequences to the life of themselves or how what they are doing will affect others. They are just lost in the moment of getting what they hope for.

Again, look back at your own life situations. Be truly honest with yourself. Why did you do what you did?

You can take this a little bit deeper if you have the mind to do so. Think about a time you did something to help someone, but the consequences to your life were not what you expected. What did you expect? Why did you expect that outcome? What was your motivation for doing what you did in the first place? And, did you ever even think about the grander scheme of reality, and how your actions may affect that reality?

What occurred and why? Really, trace it down.

Now, take a look at an action you did that you knew may hurt someone. Why would you do such a thing? What gave you the right? Be honest with yourself. What happened next and why? And, aren't you the one to blame?

The thing is, most life actions really lead to nothing. At least nothing that will be all that remembered. But, to each individual, there are those small things that take place in their life, that no one else, or few people, will ever even know about. Yet, it sets a course of events into motion. Then what?

I know from my own personal perspective; I always try to keep everything I do on the positive. I've even taken some hard shots in life for being of that mindset, because everyone else is not like that. Most, only see things through their own eyes and they are out to win, no matter the cost or the price to others. But, as far as I am concerned, that is not a good mind space to be operating from.

So, is there an answer to all of this? Is there a way to make your life consequence free? I don't think so, as there are so many unpredictable variables with everything you do. The one thing I can say is, do the best you can do to do the best you can do. Never do anything that may intentionally hurt anyone. Never do anything that you know is wrong. And mostly, take that someone else into consideration. Do that, even if it does not allow you to come out on top.

Though we can never be sure of the what comes next, with any action we take, at least if we are doing what we are doing from a selfless and helpful state of mind, any negative repercussions we may encounter will be kept to a minimal.

CHOPSTICKS
08/Jul/2025 08:05 AM

Being born into the late 1950s, and growing up through the 1960s, in a city like L.A., I have experienced a vast array of culture influences throughout my life. I guess it was when I was about six that I asked my mother to buy me a set of chopsticks.

Now, let me say right here and right now, I am not trying to cast any shade on anyone or anything when I use the term, *"Chopsticks."* I understand that some feel that it is a culturally inappropriate term. But, instead of having to state what I am speaking about in the native term from each Asia culture, I will use this understood term. If it bothers you, sorry!

I was watching an old Chuck Norris movie on the video tape. Chuck Norris, a great guy and a truly revolutionary figure in the world of the modern martial arts. But, I was reminded of how poorly he used chopsticks, at least in that movie. ...Like he really didn't know how.

Now, like when I first saw the film, (I remember), I was thinking how did he not learn how to properly use them when he was stationed in South Korea in the U.S. Military, while becoming one of the first Caucasians to study the, (then), newly developed modern Korean martial arts?

I think to how my lady, (of South Korean descent), commonly exclaims to her family members, when they make a comment about how properly I can use the chopsticks. *"He uses them better than me!"* I really don't know why that is. It's just something that I do. But, there is no competition or award for any of that.

Again, I was about six when I got my first set of chopsticks. I remember, as a young boy, trying to figure them out. I don't know why I asked for a set? I guess it was that Asian culture was never far from me. My first girlfriend, (as I jokingly refer to her), was this chubby girl of Japanese descent. We used to walk home together, at least part of the way, from our Southcentral L.A. grammar school. My best friend/first friend, from first grade was a boy of Chinese heritage. Plus, I began training in the martial arts, from a man of South Korean descent, who made his primary living as a gardener, when I was six. So… I don't know??? You put the numbers together…

In any case, I worked with the chopsticks with little thought, from the time I was very young.

A story that I believe needs retelling… At least in term of the chopsticks. …A story I have told in some form of literature, in some book, somewhere… But, one I have not written about in a long-long time. A story you may find interesting, as this is story of how the mind can be the architect of reality.

My mother's mother, my grandmother, passed away in 1967. My mother went back to the funeral in her mother's hometown in the Midwest. When she returned to L.A., she was all fake wearing her sunglasses at night, pretending to be crying, and all of that kind of stuff. I could see the BS in it then, even as a child. That's just the kind of person that she was.

The moment she came back, she began to tell the tale of how there was rain during the funeral of her mother. And, according to Scottish superstition, if there is rain on an open grave, another family member will die within a year.

…Me, I love the rain. I think that would be a good omen. But, anyway…

From that point forward, my mother would constantly remind me, (and other family members), of this fact. She continued to exclaim, *"I am the one that will die!"*

As a kid, that obviously, freaked me the fuck out. I would call out, *"No mom, don't die!"* But, she would not stop her rants.

Close to a year later, my mother, father, and I went to this Chinese restaurant over on Crenshaw to have dinner.

I, of course, wanted to eat with chopsticks. Back then, they were not passed out with every meal, as they are today. Then, you actually had to ask for them. ...Ask for them in a Chinese restaurant.

Anyway, we ate our dinner and that was that. Me, with chopsticks and my parents with a knife and fork. Afterwards, as has long been the case in Chinese restaurants, we were given our fortune cookies. My mother opened hers, and there was nothing inside of it. No fortune. *"You see,"* she exclaimed. *"I am going to die."* Immediately, my father handed her his, *"Here, take mine."*

My father died about a week later from a massive heart attack at the age of (only) forty-eight.

So, there are a lot of things you can read into this. Read into this, if you have the mind. Did her magical thinking and superstition and constant reciting of that mantra bring a curse into reality? Did her constant invocation of negativity bring about a death? Or, was the superstation true? This occurrence was and is definitely something I still, all these decades later, question?

I remember I was filming a movie with a friend of mine, just after the L.A. riots of 1992, and we ended up over and in front of that restaurant, as that area was one of the epicenters of where the riots took place and we were getting some second-unit stuff for a film we were putting together. I told him the story of that story. I remember the shocked looked in his eyes. But, that's the reality of this reality. People conjure up all kinds of life realities that have no definition in true understanding. Yet, they conjure them up just the same.

My mother, eventually coming to know who and what she was, I understand she didn't really mean to bring that reality of death onto my father. But, she was just one of those lost souls, lost into a selfish reality where she lived and project all things from a mindset of ME—hoping to keep the focus of all those that lived and surrounded her, focused on her.

So, keep this in mind the next time you evoke some level of negativity. Keep this mind, as you emphasize a superstition. Keep this mind, as you never know whose life it will take. The person who is invoking the crisis, or the person who says, *"Here, take mine."*

As for chopsticks... I'm always surprised when someone doesn't know how to use them properly. Chuck Norris or anyone else. This is the modern world, where cultures are so cross-cultured that it is hard to see the division.

Be the bridge, not the division. And mostly, do not bring your superstitions into reality for they can truly kill people and destroy the lives of those who live on.

THE WORDS YOU NEVER SAY
08/Jul/2025 08:04 AM

Have you ever had the sensation where you are thinking about a subject and you remember a friend from a time gone past—a friend that you have not been in contact with for a number of years. And, it comes to your mind—you think about discussing the subject with that person?

Maybe this is due to what you are thinking about, (or encountering), is based upon something the two of you shared as a common interest. Maybe it is based upon something that you used to do together with that individual. Or, whatever… Whatever the case, the thought of that person comes to your mind, and, for that moment, you think about sharing what is taking place with them.

I always find it very interesting in life how time and life goes on. Some people you know, you keep in your life. Most, however, they are there for a time and then they are gone.

Maybe they are there in your life for a week, a month, a year, or many years. They are there. You are friends. But then, based upon an untold amount of whatevers, they are gone from your life. They are gone. But, of course, you remember them.

I've encountered people that have reached out through the past. Why they do this is known only to them. Some, I get. Others, I do not.

I've known a couple of people that have tried to do stupid things like contact an old girlfriend. That's just ill-advised and wrong. They've got their own life now. If they wanted you in it, they would be in touch with you. All that does is to stir up shit in that old girlfriend's life and the person making the contact looks like a loser.

Some contacts are not so dastardly, however. I've been hit up by some people out of my past and it was a nice remembrance. Most of these re-contacts went nowhere, however. But, it does provide for some interesting life curiosity.

But, that's not really the point to all of this… Or, maybe it is???

The thing is, through time/via time, people change. If they are of the mind, they evolve. They have changed and they are no longer the person they once were: physically or mentally.

Have you ever seen a recent photo of someone you knew way back in the way back when and you are shaken by how much they have physically changed? That's a weird one, I know.

Time goes on, and what was back then, is not now.

And, I guess, that's what all of this is about. When you are thinking of that person, you are thinking of the individual you once knew. But, are they that same person? Are they whom you used to know? Or, have they changed? Have you?

Ultimately, who are you contacting? The person that is locked in the memories of your mind? Or, the individual they currently are/who they have become?

It's a weird thing that happens. That thinking of that someone and imagining having a conversation about something that is going on in your life, right now. Right now, when you knew them so long ago.

ARE YOU RETIRED?
07/Jul/2025 07:40 AM

    A couple of funny things I encountered over the past couple of days...

    The other day, I was driving home, and I noticed a license plate on a car that said, *"TOAD WAR."* That made me smile. I don't know??? I probably doubt it... But, was that in reference to the Zen Film??? One way or the other, it was a strange/interesting one.

    I had a personal plate on my car for a number of years. For those of you who know, you know what it was. But eventually, I realized that I prefer the anonymity of driving through traffic with nothing really to take notice of. So, I let it go. I still have the plates stuffed away behind some stuff on a shelf in my kitchen. But, that's not really any part of this tale.

    The other funny/interesting thing that happened to me is that I went into this store that I pop into every now and I got to momentarily speaking to this one young lady who works there. She asks, *"Are you retired?"* Wow, that hit me like a ton of bricks. People generally think I'm younger than I am. But, to be asked that question.

    In fact, and in truth, I guess by the standards of society, I have reached, or passed, that age. But...

    I guess that's the goal of many; isn't it? To retire. To get away from the drudgery of whatever job it is they are doing, year after year. But, that is a thought that never even crossed my mind.

    Though, I imagine, some would say that I should retire. But, my answer to the Shop Girl, *"You don't retire from what I do."*

    I mean, I never stop thinking about creating and being and... Pretty much my every thought is about the what I can do next, how can I make this Life Space better, and what can I give back to the world; via art, music, philosophy, or whatever…

Anyway, this is just a story with no dramatic or climatic ending. Just a tale to tell.

But, it may give you a pause for a thought. What does retirement mean to you? What would your life look like if you stopped doing what you are doing? What would you become? What would your life become? And, what would you do with your time?

WHAT WOULD HAVE HAPPENED IF THAT WOULD HAVE HAPPENED?
06/Jul/2025 03:01 PM

Think about a time when a situation was presented to you. A moment when you were given the choice to do something, but you did not do it. Maybe this was something very small, or maybe this was something very big. But, for whatever reason, you remember that moment and occasionally it will come to your mind. A crossroads was presented to you, and you choose to walk one path but not the other.

Bring that situation clearly into mental focus, really think it through. You most likely will remember why you choose not to do it.

Maybe at that point in time you had your reasons. Maybe as you look back you understand those reasons. Maybe when you look back you cannot understand why you made the choice you did. Maybe you have always regretted doing what you did and not doing what you didn't do. But, the fact of the fact is, that was the choice you made.

Continue along this thought process and calculate what would or could have possibly happened to you then, and to your later life, if you had made that other choice. ...If you had chosen the other road to walk down. What would that have meant to your life? How would your life have been affected? How would your life have been changed? What would it possibly have meant to your life evolution?

Obviously, this mind exercise is all based in fantasy. And, you really need to be careful walking down the path of fantasy, as fantasy is never reality. But, more than that, what was then, can never be what is now. And, for most of these life situations, based in the what was, there is no possible way to relive that choice you made and actually make a different decision.

This being understood, what this thought process—this pathway of reliving the what did not happen will allow you to do is to trace the what might have been, based upon the what never was.

It's essential to note, however, as all this is based in fantasy, whatever you think or believe might have happened will most likely never have actually been what would have occurred. So again, you need to be careful in following this thought exercise. But, what it can provide you with is an insight into your desired outcome. An outcome that never took place. The first step in the next step is, from all of this, ask yourself, why do you still hold onto to that desired outcome that did not come to be? Again, with all this as an understood basis, take a moment and really chart through the decision you made. Clearly articulate to yourself why you made the choice you did. What caused you to turn right instead of turning left?

Now that you understand your logic in making the decision you made, why has that choice continued to raise questions in mind? Why do you question the choice that you made? Again, really think this through. Why has that situation continued to pop up in your brain?

Can you find the answer to those questions?

If you can, does that give you any peace in the choice you made over the choice you could have made? If it does, great! If not, why not?

Life is a pathway of choice. At every moment of our life there is a choice that we can make. Some of those choices we understand. Some of those choices we are grateful that we made. Sometimes, we totally regret the pathway we choose to walk. Or, with other choices, we always question the what might have been. That's just life.

The main thing to understand, as you walk the path of life, is that there will be choices. And, in some cases you will believe that you made the right choice while in others you will be believe you made the wrong choice. Knowing this, all we are left with is the what's next. So, what is next based upon the choice(s) you have made?

You can choose or you can choose not to choose, that is your choice. But, from every choice, all you are left with is the consequences of that choice you made. What choice are you going to make next? And, what will that choice mean to the rest of your life? Will you always be thankful for making that choice? Or, will you always regret having made that choice.

Remember, a choice lasts forever.

A choice can make or break your life.

There is always a price to pay for every choice you make.

Your life, your choice.

* * *
06/Jul/2025 07:09 AM

When you feel bad about something that you've done, that does not change what you've done.

Now what?

* * *
06/Jul/2025 07:06 AM

What do you do when you're falling asleep, you know you need some sleep, but you don't like the dream that is projecting on the screen of your mind?

* * *

05/Jul/2025 11:33 PM

The critic will never be remembered.

Why?

Because they are not creating something artistic or unique of their own.

All they are doing is speaking about what someone else has created.

The more a critic speaks of what someone else has created, the more they lock that creator into the annals of history, and the more they remove themselves from creating something of their own.

HURT NEVER HELPS
05/Jul/2025 01:19 PM

As has been long documenting, (forever), those people who are abused, become the abusers. Those people who have been hurt, are the ones who hurt others. It's pretty easy to see, all you have to do is look around at society— look at those you have known, and you can observe those who have been on the wrong side of this equation and have been damaged by the words and the hands of others.

When you look out to the world, you see it all the time. People who are saying and doing hurtful things. Though they may each have a reason for doing what they do, if you take the time to ask them their reason why, that reason/their logic is rarely based upon the truth of the truth, rather it is simple based on their excuses for who they have become and why they feel justified in what they are doing.

Nothing new here... I'm not saying anything new. But, what I am stating is what very few people ever consciously take the time to think about before they unleash the pain.

In the digital world, where there are seemingly no consequences, people have unleashed all kinds of hurtful words and actions. Most have gotten away free and clear. But, do they/do you ever consciously take the time to calculate why they are doing what they doing which is, quite obviously, based in negativity. In fact, think of all of those who have supposed, got behind, and cheered on those who unleash negativity.

Think of all the statements that are made, the comments that are posted, the proclamations that are instigated... All based on what? Answer: Some negative something.

Even more importantly, look to your own life in the Real Life. How many people do you know that behave in this manner? How many have unleashed pain via their words and/or their actions? Do you?

It is easy to see the causation factor for what a person does. All you have to do is to chart their actions back to their source.

For example, there have been a couple of people I have known since they were very young. They, like I, had a fairly messed up childhood. Though we each were formed by our childhoods, and we each reacted to our childhood, they, unlike me, never tried to fix themselves. Here's where the true makings of a man, (or a woman), comes in play. Yes, you were formed by your experiences. If they were based in negativity, yes, you may turn on the re-play and emanate those known experiences and unleash them onto others. Or, you can be the MORE and change the pattern. Yes, it is hard; very hard. But, it can be done.

So, take a moment right now and look at yourself. Look that those you associate with; both in the world of true reality and of the digital, what do they do? Does what they do originate from a place of goodness, truth, and rightness? Or, does it come from a place of negativity and hurt and misdirected retribution, emanating from what was, (once upon a time), done to them?

Look at yourself. Whom have you hurt with your words, deeds, and actions? And, have you ever truly looked deep into this reality? Have you ever looked at what you have done through the eyes of the person you have done it to?

Truly dig deep into that place of blatant honesty, and chart your reason for doing what you did; behaving in the manner that you did and affecting the life of that someone else in the way that you did. Have you created another monster like yourself? Have you sent another person down the pathway of reflecting hurt and negativity and badness, causing harm to the life of others based upon your instigation? Mostly, ask yourself, right now, how honest you are being with yourself about this subject?

So many people justify what they do because they feel they have the right—be that right based in their ability to overpower another person in the sense of physicality or from far via their words or their hidden deeds. Some people simply believe they possess the right to judge others. And, if they don't like the words or actions of that someone else, SMASH, here comes the hit, simply because they believe that other person is wrong, and they are right. Some people are simply just so vain and misdirected that they do what they do with little or no consciousness of their actions. Thus, they damage the life of someone else without even being aware of what they are doing.

At its root, we can all agree hurt only equal hurt. We can all understand that judgement is simply someone believing someone else is wrong based upon their own limited understandings of what that someone else is saying or doing. But, in all of that Mind Junk, if pain is unleashed, what is the ultimate result? Pain, equally damage.

So, who are you? What are you? Are you the instigator of pain? If you are, and you do it either from a very cognizant or unconscious perspective—if you have unleashed the pain, based on whatever you can attribute your actions to, what have you done? Have you made the world a better place? Have you made the life of that other person, on the receiving end of your pain, any better? Or, have you simply caused more pain and, thus, re-instigated the path of further pain?

Really, who and what are you? Really, who are what are the people you associate with? Really, are you making this world a better or a more pain-filled place?

Your ability to cause pain; no matter what justification you attribute your ability to do so, is not based in the betterment of anything. At best, it is based in your physical ability, your judgmental mind, or your misdirected logic. Hurt never helps.

* * *

03/Jul/2025 07:37 AM

You can't help everybody, but you can help somebody.

Do something today that makes a positive difference in the life of an individual.

*   *   *
02/Jul/2025 12:53 PM

The more cluttered your life, the harder it is to accomplish anything.

The harder it is to accomplish anything, the less you achieve.

The less you achieve, the less you become.

IN YOUR OWN MOMENT
BUT THAT'S NO ONE ELSE'S MOMENT
01/Jul/2025 01:22 PM

You know, in Spiritual, New Age, and Positive Thinking Circles, one of the things that is often discusses is that one should stive to be in their own moment. To truly live what they are doing to this fullest. That sounds like a good thing; right?

I mean, certainly we can all attest to the fact that when we are fully engulfed in our moment, living our best life, we feel totally alive and that great sense of fulfillment is omnipresent.

Lord knows, I've spoken and written a lot about this subject; in its various forms.

But, there's a whole other level to this. That level is when one person is totally alive in their own moment, but their own moment is infringing on someone else's. Then what?

As I live in L.A., and driving is the name of the game, I am so often confronted with the realities of life, both good and bad, when I am behind the wheel.

So often, I will be driving somewhere, and I end up behind someone one who is simply lost in their own moment. Maybe they are talking to someone. Maybe they are messing around on their phone. Maybe they are playing with their screen, for the cars that have one of those. And, all of that kind of stuff. They are totally engulfed, living their own moment, but in living their own moment, they are fucking up the moment(s) of someone else.

I'm using driving as an example, as I'm sure a lot of you can relate to that situation. But, this supposed state of mind-full-ness is actually leading to a state of mind-less-ness about the anybody else. And, this goes on all the time, all over the place, in all of life situations.

The question must then be asked, if you living in your own moment is negativity affecting the life of someone else, can that be a good thing? Or, is that simply selfishness? Is that simply you not caring about the greater whole of humanity or the world?

Here's a sad fact of the world, most people couldn't care less about you, how you are feeling, or why you are feeling it. Most people couldn't care less if they are messing with your life, as long as they are feeling good about their life.

Is that you? Is that the person you are? When you are totally entrenched in your moment, are you even thinking about how that absoluteness is affecting anyone else?

There's nothing that you or I can do to change the trajectory of human reality. People are a selfish breed. The one fact is, however, you don't have to be that person. You don't have to be that somebody, that no matter how much you are in your moment, you negativity affect the life of someone else.

Keep this in mind the next time you find yourself completely submerged in your moment. Keep the question on our lips, is my being in my moment hurting the moment of anyone else? Because, if it is, all you may have gained by being in the now will be affected by the negative karma you are creating by damaging the life of that someone else.

* * *
01/Jul/2025 01:21 PM

How much of your life is spent doing the things that you have to do verses how much of your life is spent doing the things that you want to do?

*   *   *
01/Jul/2025 08:42 AM

No matter where in your life you believe you are traveling to, you are not going to actually know where you arrived until you reach the end of your road.

8-TRACK TAPE
29/Jun/2025 07:36 AM

For any of you who know me, or truly know of me, you know I'm a junky for sound. I just love listening for and studying the subtitles of sound. Not just man-made sound, but the sounds of nature, the sounds of everything...

My 8-Track player bit the dust a little while back. I decided it was time to buy another one. So, I went on the quest and ended up on eBay. I found one that claimed it was, *"Working great,"* so I bought it.

I know... I know... You have to be careful on eBay. If it says, *"Untested,"* what that really means is that it is not working. If it says, *"Lights up. But..."* That means it is not working. If it says, *"I have no way to test it."* That means it is not working. Then, there are those, like the one I purchased that said, *"Working..."* But...

Anyway, I had a pretty good day yesterday. Did a bunch of the stuff that my lady likes to do. Her, not me. But, it was a full day. I get home and there it is. All wrapped up in a big box.

I take it in. Open up the box. Plug it in. It does power up. Okay... So, I move it over to one of stereo systems. I hook it up to my vintage Marantz receiver. I grab one of my 8-Tracks tapes. One that was on the top of the pile. Bob Dylan, *The Times They Are A-Changin.* I pop it in. The motor starts up. But, nana. No sound. I tried to pull out the tape. But, the machine total grinded it. Fuck! That was a perfect condition, original release, 8-Track tape.

I try other tapes and hooking it up through different stereo system. It powers on but it does not work!

Now, I imagine a lot of you out there do not even know what an 8-Track tape is, as you are too young. If you do know, I would guess that you don't have any, as these machines are old and where popular in the later 60s and into the 70s. But, they have not made the decks for decades.

For me, as stated, I'm a sound junkie. I love the way music is presented in all forms. It is all very different. Even when I was young, I would take notice of how say an LP sounded compared to 8-Track or cassette or radio or whatever. So, all of this is my fault. I am the one, (perhaps wasting my time), seeking out a means to hear sounds from a tape system created in the past.

I had the idea, a little while back, to watch all of the Mission Impossible movies in order. I started doing that last night with MI 1. The first thing I noticed is the acting. For some, it was so much less believable than the actor they became. So much more contrived. I didn't initially realize it, but that movie was made thirty years ago. Time and everything has changed so much since then. When they were filming MI 1, I was filming, *Max Hell Frog Warrior*. Whose life do you think I wish I lived, Tom's or mine?

But, that's the thing about time. In time, it all changes. Life, people, certainly technology. With that, something is lost, while a lot more is gained. For the something lost, there are the people like me who try and hold onto some of it. Stupid, I guess. A waste of time and money, for sure.

In all things lost, there is something gained. So says the old saying. But also, in all things gained, there is something that is lost. Like stated in the Tao Te Ching, *"For the man of the world, everyday something is gained. For the man of Tao, everyday something is lost."*

So, the world or the Tao, we are each lost somewhere between the two. Where are you?

I SAVED THE LIFE OF A CAT
27/Jun/2025 06:45 AM

I saved the life of a cat the other night.

To tell the story... My lady and I were sitting around and watching TV. You may, or may not have heard about this, but, the coyote population, across the greater L.A. and Orange County region, has grown vastly. They are all over the place. Even at places you wouldn't expect like across some of the beaches.

I'm all about nature and life and all of that good stuff. But, the problem has arisen that this vast, and ever-growing population of coyotes, they need to eat. So, they have been attacking pets and, even in a couple of cases, small children.

There's a field behind where I live. And, every now and then you hear the coyotes going wild, howling, etc.

The other night, like I said, we were sitting around watching TV and I hear them start to go wild. I also could hear that a cat was in a battle for its life in the middle of them. I couldn't see any of this. It was dark. But, I could hear it. ...The coyotes going nuts and the cat hissing and scrapping and... A group of them probably had it cornered.

It was upsetting.

I said to my lady, *"I wish there was something I could do about this."*

Then, out of nowhere, it came to me. I got up, walked over to the window, and clapped my hands very loudly one time. It all stopped. The coyotes stopped howling, and the cat stopped doing all of that cat kind of stuff. I believe what I did was to distract them for that second which gave the cat time to escape.

I felt better and I am sure the cat did as well.

I've said this before, I do not know why people let their cats roam wild. No matter where you live, it is not safe and their life-time is drastically reduced. This is especially the case when there are coyotes in the neighborhood.

But, the bigger lesson to learn here is that, in life, sometimes all you need to do is to distract the attacker, even if just for a second, and this gives the victim the chance to get away.

Think about this. Think about this the next time you hear some one of some thing in distress. If you can just give them that moment of distraction, you may just save their life.

ART FOR ART SAKE
AKA HOW DO YOU BECOME AN INFLUENCER?
25/Jun/2025 08:58 AM

Just for the record here… I have never made a movie with the intention of making money from it. Every film I have ever made was created with art at its heart—and that was the only reason for its creation; at least in my mind. Did you know that about me?

This has been much the same with all of the endeavors that have come to define the life of Scott Shaw.

Did you know that I never made a dime from teaching the martial arts for all of those years I was a professional martial arts instructor? Nope… Nada. Zero. I never charged my students to be their teacher.

Now, don't get me wrong, we all need money to survive and pay our bills. And, I have done things to make money. I wasn't born with a silver spoon in my mouth. I grew up in the gutter of L.A. But, at the heart of my intention, for all of the various forms of the things that I've done that may be defined as art, it was always all about the creativity and not about the making money.

This blog, I'm asked, do I make money? Nope. It's always been free. No ads, no nothing.

My Zen Films on YouTube, not monetized, so you don't have to watch those intrusive ads. Free!

But, it all equals no dinero. My fault, I know!

You know, as this world of Influencers and Content Creators has erupted, it has always intrigued me as how some of these people have made a shit ton of money off of what they do. Now, I'm not speaking so much about say the film reviewers, and people who fall into that category, as all they are doing is telling other people what they think about someone else's creation. I'm more referencing the people who either do some interesting something on camera, but more specifically, just talk to the camera about what they are thinking and feeling.

Through the Internet Years this process has gone in various directions. I think my old *Zen Filmmaking* Buddy, Donald G. Jackson would have been great at that as long before this craze hit the airwaves, he was always having people either follow him around filming his life and his talking or when the video cameras got smaller, he would carry one around with him and film himself. I'm just not that vain to want to be that seen. But, isn't the at the heart of what these, *"Influencers,"* do; film themselves talking about whatever it is they want to talk about? And, they make money from it! I wish I knew how.

I think one of the interesting things about the various characters that come into your (my) feed on FB, IG, TikTok, and elsewhere is that sometimes it is so random. I'm told this is all based on some kind of algorithm going on and all of that kind of stuff. But, all of that is way beyond my ability to control. So??? In any case, people come into your feed. But, then they go away.

Recently, this one young lady has popped up and she is very curiously interesting. The way she talks about her mind-set is truly unique. She says all this stuff about her-self and hoping to live her best life, but really, she is saying nothing. It's like Spoken Word or abstract poetry. It's quite an ART form.

I guess she gets followers and from that makes money. Me, I spend all this time writing these blogs and there is that crew of you out there who reads them, *"Thanks!"* But, is does not equal a dime.

…And, I guess that's the thing about art, creativity, or whatever you want to call it… Or, perhaps better put, about the artist, as it's long been known most do not make any money.

I wish I knew how to become an Influencer and make money by just talking into the camera about how I feel and what I think; my philosophies and all of that kind of stuff. That would be cool. To make money and to not have to ask people to pay for anything. But, I just do not know how it is done???

DIRTY DEEDS
24/Jun/2025 07:03 AM

    Over the past couple of years, Netflix has released a few documentaries dealing with a person or persons who has done some dirty deeds, (done dirt cheap), to some person or peoples. In a few of these docs, it has involved situations in and of the internet and content creators who got screwed over.

    No matter what the medium, (internet of not), I believe it is always a sad state when someone says or does anything bad that hurts the life of someone/anyone else. Don't you feel the same way? This is especially the case when it involves children or adolescents, as it does in this most recent doc I have been viewing. I always scream, *"Leave the kids alone!"*

    As we all know, the internet is this undefined/uncharted playground. There are all these things going on. Some people, since its inception, have found a way to make it a high paying cash earner. While others have had their lives destroyed by it—even after they earned a lot of cash.

    Though I was part and parcel of watching the internet evolve. I was ridings its train since it began. But still, I have very little true knowledge about its inner-workings. Sure, I've had my website(s) up forever. And sure, I've dove deep into some of the platforms. But, I've never made any large sums of money or anything like that. And, when someone has attacked me online, I've never really saw any recourse.

    Though some of the other docs I've seen, that involve the internet, have portrayed how the lives of some people have been destroyed, more so than the one I am currently watching, it is still very clear the pain that can be unleashed. And, I've spoken about this in the past.

    It's kind of like one of those things, if you don't know about it, (the harsh words or the damage or the whatever), then, you don't know about it. Ignorance is bliss. But, if you do. You see/you know the pain it has instigated.

I've mentioned her in the past, but I knew this one sweet young lady whose boyfriend began to trash her online after they broke up and a lot of people, believing his lies, went after her. She wasn't very strong, and she took her own life. Very sad. Whatever happened to that guy, I don't know. But, his karma, leading to his destiny, has to be very-very dark.

In all of these docs, and in the life experiences I have experienced, the people doing the bad stuff have their motivations. Isn't that always the case of life? People do what they do either not taking the other person into consideration or not caring about the damage they cause as long as they get whatever it is they want.

Okay... We all know this kind of negative whatever, via the internet, goes on. But, here's the thing... Yes, there are bad people who say and do bad things. That has always been the case of life. But, you do not have to be one of them. You do not have to be the person that takes or partakes or hurts.

I know, in my life, when someone has done something positive to turn the tides of negativity around, I am always very thankful. Whether I know them or not, or ever will personally know them or not, I forever hold an appreciation for their actions. And, this should be the model for all of us. Don't not partake in the hate.

We can only do so much to control the world out there. But, the one thing that we do have control over is to make everything we do based in the positive, the helpful, the caring, and never the hurting or the negative.

So, let's keep this as our mantra, *"Help not hurt."*

When you see or hear something negative going on, on the internet or elsewhere, don't let yourself get sucked into it. Avoid it! And, if you can, turn it around with some positive words or actions. Because positivity, caring, and good always makes everything better. Remember, *"Help not hurt."*

*   *   *

23/Jun/2025 09:36 AM

If no one told you about heaven, would you still be trying to get there?

If no one told you about hell, would you still be trying not to end up there?

* * *
23/Jun/2025 09:32 AM

How much wisdom will you consume today?

A WORLD OF HURT
22/Jun/2025 03:24 PM

    Take a moment right now and think about someone that you hurt. Don't dismiss this exercise. Truly, take a moment right now and consciously visualize the hurt you have caused someone else.

    Don't lie to yourself and pretend that you have not hurt someone. Don't erase them from this process by you believing that they deserved it or anything like that.

    Take a moment right now and think about someone that you hurt. Bring what you did to them very consciously into focus.

    Now, expand this thought process. Think about other people that you have hurt. Truly, how many people have you hurt? Have there been a lot? What did you do to them?

    Now, that you have at least some of these examples in your mind, ask yourself, *"Why did you hurt them?"* Truly work through this. Did you do it consciously? Did you do it because you wanted to hurt them, (for whatever misplaced reason you may have possessed)? Did you do it because you were uncaring or unthinking about their feelings? …Because you just didn't care if they hurt? Or, did you do it by accident?

    Again, how many people have you hurt? Have there been a few or a lot?

    Once you did hurt them, how did that make you feel? Did you feel sorry? Did you feel sad that you hurt them? Did you care at all? Did you feel justified? Did you feel empowered? Did You feel good about yourself? Did you take pride in your ability to hurt that other person? But, more importantly, now that you are taking a conscious note of how you felt, how do you feel about how you felt?

    Why do I suggest that you bring these hurtful actions, on your part, into mental focus? Because few people ever think about the pain they cause to others. Certainly, they think about the pain they have felt when someone has hurt them. But, they rarely, if ever, think about the pain they have caused to someone else unless they are reveling in their power over that other individual. And, if someone is operating from that perspective, they are a pretty messed up individual, don't you think?

Okay, now that you have at least some of these hurtful actions in your mind, what does you hurting others, and the reason you did hurt someone else, say about the person that you are? In fact, who are you? What gave you the power or the desire to hurt anyone in the first place? Do you like it when you have been hurt? Probably not. So, this should be a game plan for what you do to others.

Now that the *"What you've done,"* is on your mind, think about this. Those people that you have hurt are only those that you are focusing on. Imagine how many other people you have hurt, throughout your life, and you did not even realize that you did hurt them. What is that number?

The reason I periodically discuss this subject is that I am frequently questioned from others about why their life is not where they want it to be, why their life did not turn out the way they hoped, why they are encountering negativity in their life, and all of that kind of stuff. My answer is always the same, *"Karma."* And, this is something that most people do not want to look at or acknowledge; namely, the actions that they took which created their own karma.

In fact, this is where a lot of people go astray in their system of belief, stating, *"I may have hurt that person but I've helped a lot of other people."* That's not how karma works. You cannot erase your bad karma, instigated from something you have done to hurt one person, by doing something good for someone else.

If you have hurt someone, you have hurt someone. It is as simple as that. If you have not fixed that damage, that damage is forever present in the life of the individual you hurt. No matter what you reason, logic, or motivation for unleashing that hurt, hurt only does one thing, it hurts. And hurt, if it is not fixed, hurts forever. Thus, your karma is forever sent in a negative direction.

Most people never wish to think about any of this. How about you? Most people never want to look at themselves for the true state of their existence. How about you? If you do not chart those you have hurt, if you do not undo that damage, what do you think should be the result to your life?

THE NEW CHURCH OF ZEN ENTERTAINMENT
20/Jun/2025 10:45 AM

I was looking through some of my previous blogs and I came upon this one that I wrote about a year ago. As I do periodically, I pull down the old blogs and then they are published in book form. You can find this one in, *Zen and the Shadow of the Flower*. Reading it, I thought that some of you may find it interesting and thought provoking. So, here it is, (again).

After mentioning DGJ in the blog yesterday, it got me to thinking about one of the events in the later stages of his life where he conceived, *The New Church of Zen Entertainment*. If you watch one of my Zen Documentaries, *Bluegrass Christmas Party,* on YouTube, you can hear him mention this church in his piece of Performance Art near the beginning of the Zen Film.

So, what was, *The New Church of Zen Entertainment* all about? I don't really know??? I don't think Don really knew either. But, he had this idea that it would be this ever-growing expansive foundation where he (we) could do pseudo-religious services, film festivals, and video productions that would be sent out to the devotees, (this was before the current state of the internet, where everything is broadcastable), all based around a central theme of the spirituality of filmmaking. Interesting idea, but nothing ever came of it.

Like Fred Olen Ray said in his <u>great</u> new book, *Hell-bent for Hollywood,* in one of his mentions of Don, "*...Don possessed an unstructured, but enthusiastic, spiritual approach to filmmaking. Everything just flowed from him. Creativity and his love of off-the-wall subjects drove him.*" Very true. But, the thing about Don was, and I've said this many times before, Don possessed what I dubbed, "*The Elvis Complex."* He really thought he was the center of the world, even though it was everyone else, i.e. me, (or other people), who were actually doing the all and the everything. He really felt he was some sort of a prophet.

Again, quoting Fred, *"Don kept shooting disjointed images. I wouldn't call them scenes. There was no sense of plot, let alone a script. He couldn't pause long enough to plan or organize a real production."* Thus, if he was a prophet, he was a prophet of chaos. And, that's not a bad thing. I believe it is true art. But, the whole Elvis Complex did sometimes bother on me.

Though these two quotes are taken a bit of context, I believe they do provide ideal insight into the mind of DGJ.

The thing about Don was, he was so scattered, that it was very hard for him to complete anything. Thus, so was the case of, *The New Church of Zen Entertainment.* It just kind of faded away.

To dive a bit deeper, Don had taken this nude photo of one of the starlets he had a relationship with—taken it and had created a poster for the church. He was paying her rent and stuff like that. Something he also did with a few of his other close female cohorts, as well. Sad, really… That's why his family and he never had any money, though he had raised millions. He gave it all away… But, the girl got pissed when she saw that she was on the poster. She didn't want to have anything to do with this, *"New Church."* Though, I will say, it was a great photograph of her.

After he passed away, Don's wife gave me that poster, which had ended up in their garage. I thought to keep it. As stated, it was a great shot and a true piece of *Zen Filmmaking* History. But, I thought I would respect the model's wishes and get rid of it. I mean, if you don't respect the other person's wishes, what is life all about?

So, why am I talking about this? Answer: I believe that it illustrates a very common mindset that dominates the life of certain people. …People who believe they have something special to offer. …Something unique and special that is not possessed by someone else.

The problem is, do they? Do they really have that, *"Something Special?"* Or, is that, *"Something Special,"* nothing more than something generated in their own mind?

I guess that's for the everyone else to decide. But, what I will say is that, someone who operates from this mindset, is operating from a mindset of ego. And, is ego ever a good place to operating from?

Whether it was Jesus, Caesar, King James, Freud, Jim Jones, Rajneesh, DGJ, or whomever, what they are claiming was only claimed by them. Some of these people, obviously, drew a massive amount of followers. One of the mentioned, did not. Yet, they each possessed the same mindset, believing that they were someone who knows something that no one else understands.

The point is, you really need to be careful with people who operate from this perspective. They are dangerous. They may take advantage of people, get others to believe in what they are propagating. And, this goes to all levels of life. From the very small talkers to the ones who scream out to the world.

In closing, be careful whom you listen to. Be watchful of the people you walk down the road with. Sure, they may have a new idea about a new something. But maybe, they are just a self-proclaiming egotist or a liar, who will lead you to disaster.

FIXING WHAT IS BROKEN
18/Jun/2025 08:04 AM

Have you ever tried to fix something that is broken? Have you ever really gone all-in and tried to make something that was broken new again?

Maybe you broke it by accident. Maybe you broke it intentionally. Whatever the case, it is not what it once was, and it needed to be repaired.

Though I am certainly not a luthier. But, there was a time when I worked on guitars a lot. I was living in this apartment in Hermosa Beach in the 80s that had this big kitchen. I had my woodworking gear all set up down at one end.

I guess I was inspired by a couple of friends that I had at the time. I mean, these guys were true guitar luthiers. I was amazed at some of the stuff I watched them accomplished. They would truly fix or repair or modify a guitar, playing with the wood in just the right way. It was truly an advanced artform.

I had this girlfriend back then. Hot Latin tempered. She got mad at me this one time and she grabbed one of my favorite guitars and totally smashed it. A 1968 Guild D55. That was the first year of that guitar model's production. So, even back in the 80s, it was a valuable instrument.

SMASH, BANG, BROKEN, GONE. All based in anger.

I believe that is one of things about The Broken. Think how many things are broken out of anger. Think how many things are broken out of unconscious action. Think how many things are broken by you just not caring about what someone else cares about. Then, once broken, how can it be fixed? Moreover, do you even care if it is or can be fixed when it is not something that you, personally, care about?

Anyway, I spent a lot of time trying to repair that guitar. But, it never came back to what it once was. ...Once was before it was broken.

And, that's another big issue. Once something is broken, in all cases, it is really hard to fix.

I was putting something away today. As I was lifting it over this table I accident banged the end of that table with it. I noticed that I chipped the corner of that table. Now, I am going to have to try and fix it.

But, think about this... If I hadn't done that. If my actions had been more precise. That table would not be broken. Thus, I would not have to try and fix it.

You know, we all break things in life. Whether we mean to or not, we are responsible for things being damaged. A good life is defined by one who breaks as few things as possible. A good life is defined by someone who breaks as few elements of another person's life as possible.

Think about your own life. What have you broken? Now ask yourself the deeper question, why did you break it? Was it based upon an accident? Was it based upon you not being conscious of what you were doing? Or, was it broken out of anger, arrogance, or whatever? Did you break it intentionally?

Let's look at the bigger question... Once you did break something, what did you do about it? If you broke something of yours, that you cared about, I imagine you tried to get it fixed. Or, maybe replace it. But, what about that somebody else's something that you broke? What did you do about that? Did you do anything?

In life, things get broken. That's just the nature of the beast. It is what you do about that Broken something, after the fact, that comes to be the definition of whom you truly are and what will be your next dose of karma.

Think about all of this for a few moments. Think about this the next time you break something: physical or personal.

Now that it's broken, what are YOU going to do next?

* * *

17/Jun/2025 01:58 PM

Most people do not attempt to make themselves the best version of themselves.

Most people do not attempt to evolve.

Most people only seek what they desire, as hidden as that desire may be.

How much time do you spend becoming the better version of yourself?

How much time do you spend diving deep into the deeper meanings of life?

While we live, all of us who are living, are walking this path together.

What are you doing to make yourself the best example of yourself while helping others along their road?

HOW MUCH WOULD YOU PAY TO BE IN A MOVIE?
16/Jun/2025 03:17 PM

Back in the days of the Scott Shaw, Donald G. Jackson *Zen Filmmaking* Alliance, we did a lot of casting. We were shooting movies all the time. …Pretty much back-to-back for a period of time. So, we were always looking for new faces and people with interesting talents or skillsets to put in our Zen Films. We met some GREAT people!

Some of the people we met were very nice. Some were very professional. Some were totally full of themselves, proclaiming that they would be a major Hollywood star tomorrow and we would be lucky to have them now. Or course, we never heard anything from or about that person again. But, it was always an interesting look into the human psychology of those walking the path of acting here in the filmmaking capital of the world, Hollywood, California. The stories I could tell you… (And, maybe already have).

One of the common things that a few of those up-and-comers would ask. …Ask before they were even cast in a film was, *"How much does it pay?"* This question always sent Don through the roof. He was always on edge about stuff like that. About people over valuing their worth.

We got to a point where we would immediately jokingly turn it around and say, *"How much are you going to pay me to put you in the film?"*

Think about this… Think about how many people would love to be in a feature film that had guaranteed international distribution as our films did. I believe everyone, somewhere deep down inside, wishes that they could be a star. How about you?

Plus, this was back in the days when making a film was still a very expensive process. Not like today, where all you need is your iPhone. But, before I get off track…

You know, in a lot of ways, this has all come full circle. I mean, think about it... Think about how many people are putting up notices seeking funding to make their movie on platforms like Kickstarter and IndieGoGo. Sure, they offer get, *"Thanks,"* credit for sending in some small amount of money. But, a bit up the financial ladder, many offer *"Be in the Film,"* for X amount of dollars.

Back in the day, it was actually illegal to do that. Sure, there were people going around the backside and doing it in hidden ways. But, you could not put an ad out there asking people to pay to be in a film. My-my, how times have changed.

When I first saw this taking place, I wondered how they did it. But, times changed, and they do...

I've never sought funding for one of my Zen Film on one of those sites. I doubt anyone would give me any money anyway. People would just rather throw shade and pay nothing.

But, here and now, it has become an entire industry, paying to be in a film or to get credit as a producer or a whatever...

So, this takes us to the pinnacle of all of this... What are you willing to do, what are you willing to pay to get what you want—to become what you hope to become? And, here's the deeper question, if you have not reached that goal in your life is it because you have not paid the price, or have not paid the right people to get you where you ultimately want to be?

   * * *

16/Jun/2025 07:21 AM

How much of what you say is based upon what someone else has said?

If what you say is based upon what someone else has said, what do you owe that person for saying it first?

BUDDHA SAID
15/Jun/2025 03:11 PM

Buddha Said before you speak let your words pass through three gates.

Gate One: Is what you are saying true?

Gate Two: Is what you are saying necessary?

Gate Three: Is what you are saying kind?

How many things have you said in your life that did not follow this pattern?

What are you going to do about it?

BUY ME A DRINK
15/Jun/2025 07:08 AM

Somebody bought me a drink yesterday. It was kind of a strange experience, as I cannot tell you the last time anyone has bought me a drink.

To tell the tale, my lady and I went into this new restaurant to have dinner. They sat us down, all good. There was an elderly couple sitting at the table next to us, but no big deal. Right about then, the son and/or the daughter (I guess) of this couple came to sit down. With them, they had two very small children. One was a baby, and the other was maybe a year or so old. They were trying to squeeze in and get situation. I knew they were not going to have an enjoyable dining experience, dealing with all of that and my lady and I sitting so close. You know how most modern restaurants are now, they put the tables way too close together. I hate that!

Anyway, I saw an empty table behind us, grabbed our menus, and told them we were going to move. No big deal. They thanked us and that was that. The server came and moved our original table next to them, so they had more space. Great!

When the server came over to our new table a few minutes later, he also brought us two glasses with a shot of white wine in each. *"We just got this new wine in, and it's very good. I thought you might like to try it"* I do not believe that has ever happened to me. The waiter bringing a glass of wine to test before my asking for it. I mean, a lot of people don't drink alcohol. But and anyway, though I'm not a big fan of white wine, it was pretty good, so, *"Sure, why not."* I ordered two glasses.

We ate our meal. Drank our wine. He brought the check. I threw down my credit card, never looking at the bill. I never do. Though I suppose I should because there have been a few times in the past when I have not and later my lady has realized they have over charged me/us. But, anyway...

The gentleman came to run my card, and he said, *"They paid for your wine."* Wow! I guess as a gesture of thanks for our moving, they pick up the bill for the two glasses of wine. That was very nice. In fact, I was floored by it. It seems like people never do anything nice anymore. Never do something nice, just to do something nice.

I'm thinking back and the last time I can think of that anyone ever bought me a drink just to do it. It was this one time, a number of years deep now. I was in this sleazy bar. I was with my sweet little side-piece at the time. She was this exotic young thing from the far side of India. The thing was, she was only twenty. And here, in Cali, you have to be at least twenty-one to drink in a bar. But, knowing this place, and them knowing me, I knew no one would ask her for an ID.

Anyway, a couple of new beers came our way. This Africana gentleman, sitting at the bar, had sent them over to the booth we were inhabiting. Thanks! Didn't really want another round. Wasn't planning to drink another one, as we, (the sweet young thing and I), had already pounded down a few and I had to drive. But, it was a nice gesture. I guess??? I sent another round his direction.

Here, this restaurant, last night, I'm kinda glad that I didn't know that they had paid for the round. If I did, I would have reciprocated and sent over a bottle. But, in leaving, we both, (my lady and I), expressed our thanks to them. It was a nice gesture! And, nice gestures are all nice as nice gestures are really rare.

Okay here's the thing and the point to all of this... When was the last time you did anything nice for anyone, wishing nothing in return? I mean, it seems like whenever anybody does anything nice, they only do it because they want something from the person they are doing it for. They never just do it. Again, when was the last time you did anything nice for anyone, wishing nothing in return?

Don't you think we should change that? Don't you think you should be out there doing nice things to and for people. ...Do those things, just because.

Why don't you make it a point to do that today. Do something nice for someone, expecting nothing in return. Do it just to do it. Why don't you do that tomorrow, as well. Make it a pattern in your life. Don't you think that by operating from that perspective, it will make someone's life just a little bit better? And, from that style of behavior, don't you think that maybe the entire would/will become just a little bit better?

Like I always say, *"The world begins with you."* Do something nice for someone. Do it, just to do. What do you have to lose?

* * *
12/Jun/2025 10:35 PM

When you realize that everyone is fragile, you no longer do anything that will hurt anyone.

AND THEN IT IS GONE
12/Jun/2025 09:40 AM

A lot of people believe, (and I believe this is a very false belief), that for wine to be good, it must cost a lot of money. Long ago, I realized this not to be true.

Maybe twenty years deep now, I happened into my local Trader Joe's and noticed this bottle of Toscana, from a vineyard in Italy, of course. I grabbed a few bottles and when I tasted it that night, I was floored at just how good it was. I poured some for my lady, and she loved it too. The next day, I went back a grabbed a case.

Whenever someone would come over, I would pour them a glass. I never said anything, but the moment they tasted it, they would expressed how really good it was and where could they get a bottle (or more) for themselves. I also gave a few bottles away as gifts. Each time, the person would contact me asking where I purchased it and for how much. Answer: Trader Joe's for $2.99.

At first, no one believed me. But, they would go to their local Trader Joe's and buy their own bottle. Then, the proof was in the pudding.

I purchased that wine for a time, never thinking that it would go away. But then, one day, I purchased a bottle, not noticing that the vintage date had changed. I took it home. Opened it up later that evening, and, *"What?"* It was not the same. Checking the bottle and looking at a previous bottle I had on my wine rack, I realized that though the label was the same, this vintage had been produced in the next year. All the greatness was gone. I was so sad. It looked exactly the same. But, it was not the same.

A week or so I ago, my lady and I were in this shop in a strip mall. Next-door, this discount supermarket had just opened. We had some time to kill so we thought that we would check it out. ...Just for fun. Looking at the produce, it was the same price that it was at our local market. But, it was way poorer quality. So, no way! I'm really into fresh food. Then, we happened over by the alcohol section. We discovered they had some of these, (hard to find), what I call a slurpy alcohol-based kind of beverage, as they are ice based. My lady really likes those, so we grabbed a few. While we were there, I looked at the wine, and they had a few bottles of Pino Noir that grabbed my interested, from vineyards in California. What the heck… I grabbed four varying bottles.

Over the next couple of days, I tried each of them out. One of them was really-really good. How much did it cost? $3.99.

Me, once I experienced that taste, I had to go back to that store. I bought a case. Enjoyed it all. Then, yesterday, my lady and I were driving by the store, and I suggested that we go in. I looked and looked, but that wine was all gone. Finally, looking to the back of the shelves, I found one remaining bottle. Of course, I purchased it. Now, it sits waiting for me to drink it. But, once I do, then all of that great flavor will be gone.

And, this is the thing about all things in life, it is here and then it is gone. And, when it is gone, it is gone. There is no way to get it back.

What has left you and your life, that you can never have again? What person, place, or thing??? It was there. You loved it. But now, it is no more.

Remember, it's all going to go away: you, me, it, everything. So, love it while you can, because before you know it, it will be no more.

* * *
11/Jun/2025 08:40 AM

How quietly can you exist?

SCOTT SHAW, ZEN FILMMAKING, AND THE YOUTUBE GENERATION
10/Jun/2025 01:34 PM

How much time do you spend on YouTube? No really, how much do you spend on YouTube? I mean, there is a world of free to view Everything on that platform, as well as more how-to stuff than you or I could ever have imagined.

YouTube is really not all that old. It was launched in 2005. That's just about twenty years ago. Do you even remember life before YouTube? It is kind of hard to do so if you think about it.

Google actually had its own video platform before YouTube. But, it's gone. Why? Only the powers that be at Google can answer that. It was pretty good.

There were a couple of other sites out there, on the world wide web, before YouTube that used to focus on movies and video presentation. I remember my *Zen Filmmaking* brother, Donald G. Jackson turned me on to one site, before his untimely passing. He had uploaded his film, *Raw Energy* to it and suggested that I may want to upload one or more of my Zen Films as well. Which I did. I uploaded the first version of *Samurai Vampire Bikers from Hell.* So, if you were around back then, and you got to see it then, you were able to view a very-very rare cut of that film. But, that site is long-long gone.

There was no money to be made, on that or other similar sites, like some people now do on YouTube.

I don't make any money off of YouTube. First of all, I hate those pre and/or during video ads. So, I just don't want to put viewers of my films through any of that. And also, because a lot of my films, especially my earlier stuff, (the one's that are the most watched), are Adult Only, so you can't monetize those anyway. Plus, YouTube doesn't really pay very much. Not enough to make any difference in my life. So, why bother??? Just keep the *Zen Filmmaking* flowing for free.

The reality of life is, the days of the VHS, the DVD, and Blu-ray are over. Do you know anyone who watches any of those anymore? I don't. Not even me. Not unless I am forced to. Now, it's all about the Streaming. Thus, YouTube rules the game. ...YouTube at least for those who don't want to pay for the other more cash-involved streaming services.

But really… You can find a lot of cool, cutting-edge stuff on YouTube. Stuff that you will not see nowhere else.

So really, how much time do you spend on YouTube? If you don't spend any, you are probably a more refined soul than myself.

My generalized focus on the platform is music videos and when I need to know how to do what I need to know how to do. It's a great place to learn it. Also, I like to check out the demos of synthesizers, cameras, and the like. Mostly, there's always something to learn or to waste your Life Time while viewing.

Zen Filmmaking has a home on YouTube. But, you probably already know that. I've uploaded a lot of my and Donald G. Jackson stuff onto the platform. And, it's up there for FREE! So, if you feel like wasting some time, and maybe delving into the evolution of my style of filmmaking, you can check it out.

Or, and maybe even better yet, you can create your own cinema magic and show the world your creative skills.

YouTube, you can't live without it. Or, can you?

THE ZEN

www.ingramcontent.com/pod-product-compliance
Lightning Source LLC
Chambersburg PA
CBHW050553170426
43201CB00011B/1676